Information Technology

An Introduction

Information Technology
An Introduction

by **Peter Zorkoczy**

Knowledge Industry Publications, Inc.
White Plains, NY and London

621.38
Z88

Communications Library
Information Technology: An Introduction

First published in Great Britain 1982 by Pitman Books Ltd, London

North American edition published by

Knowledge Industry Publications, Inc.
701 Westchester Ave.
White Plains, NY 10604

Library of Congress Cataloging in Publication Data
Zorkoczy, Peter.
   Information technology.
   (Communications library)
   Bibliography: p.
   Includes index.
   1. Telecommunication.   2. Data transmission
   systems.   3. Computer networks.   I. Title.
   II. Series.
TK5105.Z67 1982   621.38   82–10115

ISBN 0–86729–037–4

Contents

Preface

This book is intended as an introduction to the current concepts, applications and tools of information technology. It is for the non-specialist in the field and does not assume a familiarity with the underlying mathematical and engineering ideas. The book is organized into two main parts; these are graded in their level of technical detail. In Part 1, Chapter 1 is about some of the fundamental concepts of information technology, in particular about information itself. Chapter 2 is about the applications of this new technology in many areas of industry, commerce, education and training, leisure, medicine and welfare. Established applications are clearly distinguished from those which, though technically feasible now, are possibilities for the future.

These two chapters are essentially descriptive in their approach. They aim to explain more *what* information technology can do, rather than *how* it is done. That latter job is reserved for Part 2. There, the important concepts and tools of information technology are given a more technical treatment, though still at an introductory level.

Part 2 includes a résumé of the three areas which form the historical basis of information technology: *computers, telecommunications* and *data networks*. A further ten chapters are devoted to the relevant technical developments which have grown out of the first three over the last few years, ranging from 'artificial intelligence' to videotex systems.

Readers who wish only to gain an impression of the scope and implications of information technology will find the first two chapters adequate for this purpose, and could use Part 2 and the general reading section as reference sources. Such readers will welcome the generous cross-referencing from Part 1 to Part 2. Readers with an interest in, but no background knowledge of, the technical aspects of information technology may find it helpful to read about computers and telecommunication systems in Part 2 first, as these form the foundation of the subject.

When writing this book I have been keenly aware that information technology is in a period of dynamic growth, accompanied by all the growing pains and uncertainties which characterize the 'adolescent phase' of a young subject. What I aimed to do, therefore, is to set out the 'family tree' of information technology, and to provide a 'snapshot' of the face it presents at the time of writing. By the time this book reaches its readers the face will have matured, but I hope the highlighted features will remain recognizable.

Peter Zorkoczy
February 1981

Part 1

1 About information technology

What's in a name?

'Information technology' is a relatively recent and perhaps not particularly well-chosen addition to the English language. It has its counterparts in the French 'informatique' and the Russian 'informatika'. For many people, 'information technology' is synonymous with 'the new technology'—the use of microprocessor-based machines: microcomputers, automated equipment, word processors and the like. But the use of man-made tools for the collection, generation, communication, recording, re-arrangement and exploitation of information goes back in time much beyond the present 'micro-revolution'. For others, the significance of the introduction of a new term, 'information technology', is the belief that the principles, practice and terminology of information handling can be treated on a unified, systematic basis. Cynics may say that the words 'information technology' simply represent an attempt to make respectable some commercially motivated developments in electronics, and politically motivated moves to control the access to information.

Whatever is the truth behind these attitudes, to qualify as a 'technology', in the sense of being 'a practice of an applied science' (*Oxford English Dictionary*), there has to be a recognized science of information. Of course, the words 'information science' have been used, and are being used, to refer to a branch of librarianship dealing with the automatic retrieval of printed documents. But to rely purely on this aspect of information handling for parentage would be too restrictive for this infant field of technology. More properly, one must look towards the science of electronic systems and to computer science to legitimize the products of their convergence.

Even these sciences have their sceptics and it will be only when the science of information reaches a maturity of its own that one can use the name 'information technology' in any more than a loose way. We shall, therefore, not formulate a precise definition at this stage, but rather attempt to illustrate by examples, and describe in terms of constituent parts, the subject that is currently taking shape under the umbrella term of 'information technology'.

The motivating forces

There is a number of reasons why information technology is becoming a subject of wide-ranging discussion and study. Each of these reasons is significant on its own, but by acting together, as they are doing at the present time, they are adding urgency to the need to understand the technical and social issues involved. From a *social* point of view, information technology promises changes in the way we communicate and reach decisions. Even in its era before the computer, progress in telecommunications—for example, telephone, radio and television—

opened out the horizons for individuals and society at large, and so placed at the disposal of people information about distant events and new ideas. This has helped us to understand some of the complexities of the surrounding world, but has in turn increased that complexity by making possible a greater degree of interaction among people.

The application of the computer to information handling has contributed a new tool and a new dimension of complexity, through its ability to store and process vast amounts of data at high speed. For many decades now, data gathering devices (e.g. measuring instruments) have increasingly extended the accessible portion of the physical world and added to the already vast stock of scientific and technical information. Improved technological tools for collecting data about people have encouraged administrative applications of information technology. However, the cost and complexity of these tools have made them the virtual monopoly of the state and of large commercial enterprises. This created a potentially threatening opportunity for highly centralized control and decision-making. Recent technological developments in microelectronics have somewhat changed this situation by reducing the price of some data handling tools and making them more widely available. But has the danger of information technology being used for increased control of peoples' lives been averted completely? The answer can be gained only through better understanding of the technology and its implications.

In parallel with the growth of information resources, there has been a significant social change: a shift in the profile of the working population towards information-related jobs. In the United Kingdom, for example, one in every three people employed in the manufacturing industries is classified as an 'administrative, technical or clerical worker', as opposed to one in every four in 1965. Table 1.1 shows the breakdown of the 11.2 million people employed in information-related industries in the UK in 1978 (out of a total working population of 22.7 million); the underlying trends are shown in Fig. 1.1.

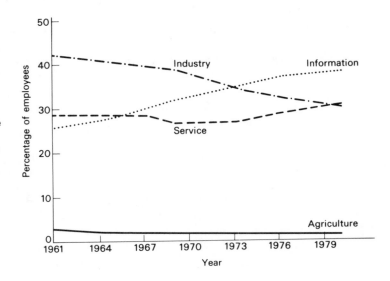

Fig. 1.1 Changes in the percentage of employees in various sectors of the economy of the United Kingdom. The information sector includes public administration, administrative, technical and clerical workers in the manufacturing industries, professional and scientific services, insurance, banking and finance. The service sector includes distributive trades, transport and communication and miscellaneous services. (Source: Department of Employment)

Table 1.1 Employment in information-related sectors in the United Kingdom 1961–1978 (Source: Department of Employment)

	Number employed (millions)	
	1961	1978
Administrative, technical and clerical staff in manufacturing industry	2.00	2.03
Distributive trades	2.76	2.74
Public administration	1.40	1.63
Insurance, banking, finance	0.68	1.15
Professional and scientific services (education, health care, communication, etc.)	2.12	3.68
Totals	8.96	11.23
Percentage of labour force (not including self-employed and the armed forces)	40.20	49.40

Note that these figures relate to employer classification, rather than employee, or occupational groups. There are no figures being issued for the latter in the United Kingdom.

In the United States, the trends are similar, as indicated by Fig. 1.2. Note that, by about 1960, more people were engaged in the handling of information than in producing food, manufacturing goods or providing services. The breakdown of the information-sector occupations (see Fig. 1.3*) indicates how the steady increase in the number of professional and technical workers, on the one hand, and managers and administrators, on

Fig. 1.2 Changes in the percentage of employees in various sectors of the economy of the United States. The information and service sectors are defined as in Fig. 1.1. (Source: US Bureau of Labor Statistics)

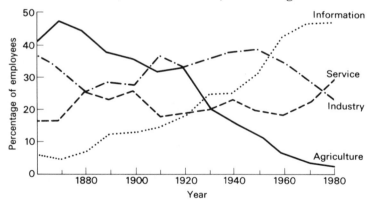

the other, has been accompanied by an increase in the number of their support staff—the clerical workers. Such social trends are not easily reversed, and there is no reason to believe that the information sector will lose its dominant position in the employment field. Information technology, then, will have a direct impact on the majority of the working population of highly developed countries.

* This occupational breakdown was first suggested by Marc Porat in *The Information Economy*, US Government Printing Office, 1977.

From an *economic* viewpoint, the data in Table 1.1 and Figs. 1.1 and 1.2 indicate a growing imbalance between traditionally 'wealth-producing' and 'overhead' occupations. At the present time, information handling is highly labour-intensive, and information workers command substantial remuneration. Yet, the value of the output of such workers is difficult to measure. How does one compare the 'output' of a teacher or a researcher with that of, say, a production-line operative?

In the absence of reliable measures of relative productivities, the traditional response of employers is to attempt to 'balance the books' in economic terms, by limiting overhead expenditures. As the most important component of this is labour costs, industry and government are turning towards information technology as a possible means of expenditure control. After all, it is argued, technology has a reasonable record in automating some production tasks; should it not be able to do the same in information handling?

What is the true cost of information? What is its market value? How does it fit into the present framework of economic decision-making? Attempts to provide answers to questions of this type furnish the second source of incentives to study information technology.

The third stimulus comes from the industries which have recently grown up around information-related products, in particular in

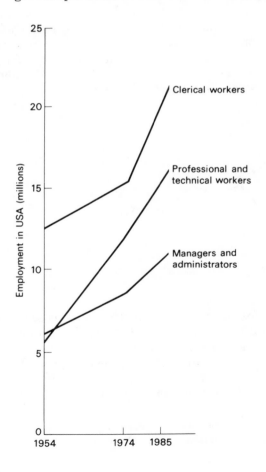

Fig. 1.3 Breakdown of the information-sector occupations in the United States, projected to 1985. (Source: *Monthly Labor Review*)

microelectronics. Manufacturers already active in the computer and telecommunication fields—the corner-stones of information technology—have now been joined by the silicon-chip industry in an attempt to open up new markets for their products: the office, the school, the publishing industry—the very places where information is in the forefront of interest. These manufacturers can be expected to turn out a vast range of products aimed at the population at large. But, to a large extent, the rapid progress in microelectronics caught the 'traditional' computer world unprepared for the greatly increased range of potential applications of its products. The engineering know-how is there, but it is still very much visible behind the thinly spread expertise on where and how to apply information technology, so that its *users* derive maximum benefit. In other words, at the present time, information technology is very much technology-led. Both the manufacturers and their customers require urgent answers to questions about the appropriateness and timeliness of various products. Such questions can be properly treated only by developing a better understanding of how the technology can complement human information handling.

Lastly, from the viewpoint of the *individual*, the possession and accessibility of information are becoming matters of personal importance. In societies made information-aware by computerization, communication technology, and shifting job patterns, the possession of information is increasingly seen as a key to professional advancement. So the control of access to information could, even more than before, become an expression of power, a weapon to be used by, or against, the individual. The growth of information technology has already given rise to concern about diminished individual freedom (see, for example, Carlson in *Information Technology Serving Society*, Pergamon, 1979). At the same time, it is placing at the individual's disposal vast resources of information, and more accessible means of voicing an informed opinion.

So, will information technology be, and be seen to be, a means towards the greater, rather than the more restricted, freedom of the individual? No answer to this question is possible without a better understanding of the technical and social issues involved and without an informed public discussion of the alternative courses of progress.

Seen from these four viewpoints—those of society, economics, technology and the individual first—the common element of information technology is the concept of *information*.

What is information?
People have a surprising range of ideas on what information is. (Just try asking a few people to define it.) Even dictionaries cannot agree. The *Oxford English Dictionary* gives it as 'that of which one is apprised or told; intelligence, news'. Another dictionary simply equates it to knowledge: 'that which is known'. Yet other definitions emphasize the knowledge *transfer* aspect of information, calling it 'the communication of instructive knowledge', or 'the knowledge conveyed to the mind by a statement of fact'.

The cause of this diversity in the common usage of the term is that information is essentially intangible: we encounter it only operationally, through its subjective effects. We *derive* information from data—from observations of the world around us. We *convey* information by communication.

'Information is the *meaning* that a human expresses by, or extracts from, representations of facts and ideas, by means of the known conventions of the representations used' (*Guide to Concepts and Terms in Data Processing*, North Holland, 1971). This is in many ways an attractive definition, but it includes the word 'meaning', which is just as intangible and elusive as 'information' (see, for example, Ogden and Richards, *The Meaning of Meaning*, Routledge & Kegan Paul, 1949). An important point, to which the last definition calls our attention, is 'the known conventions of the representations used'. When the representation is a language, as it frequently is, the syntax and the semantics of the language form an assumed supporting structure for any information expressed through it. For example, if we hear someone say, 'It is ninety-five in the shade', we can take this to mean that he is talking about temperature, that his numbers refer to degrees Fahrenheit, that the shade is not of any specific object, i.e. the temperature reading does not necessarily refer to only one place, etc. Consequently, by assuming that he employs the known conventions of the English language and culture, we can derive more information than was directly communicated by the original sentence.

The semantic and syntactic aspects of information occupy the attention of many linguists (see, for example, Bar-Hillel, *Language and Information*, Addison-Wesley, 1964), but have so far not led to a generally accepted definition of information. 'Information in most, if not all, of its connotations seems to rest upon the notion of *selection power*', Cherry tells us in his thought provoking book *On Human Communication* (Science Editions, 1961). For example, we may think of a telephone directory as containing a great deal of information because each entry selects one person or organization out of a very large number in the geographical area covered by the directory. It also links that person with a unique selection of digits (the telephone number) out of the millions of possible combinations of those digits. Moreover, the directory repeats this selection process for all the subscribers listed. The postal address given for a subscriber is also an example of the selective power of information. The address is located by a process of increasing refinement: area, town, street, house, etc.

Note that behind the selective aspect of information is the assumption of the existence of a finite, albeit large, number of alternatives which are known to *both* the originator and the user of that information. (Otherwise, the process is no longer that of selection.) Thus, in the case of names in a telephone directory, the possible alternatives are the various ways in which the letters of the alphabet can be combined. But the universe of knowables—concepts, ideas, facts, names, etc.—is practically *infinite*. This apparent impasse between what we may want to communicate and the way we communicate is resolved by separating the *content* of information from its *representation*.

The representation (symbols, signs, signals, etc.) can then indeed belong to a well-defined finite set (the alphabet, dots and dashes, etc.). The process of communication of information in that case becomes a process of communication of representations. New ideas will be communicated by new combinations of old signs. It is this totally objective way of looking at information transfer that is of interest to telecommunication engineers (and theoreticians), and lies at the basis of *information theory* (Hartley, 'The transmission of information', *Bell System Technical Journal*, 1928, p. 535; Shannon and Weaver, *The Mathematical Theory of Communication*, University of Illinois Press, 1949).

The quantity of information

Information theory quantifies information (more exactly, the signs carrying a message) as follows: it assumes that the more unpredictable the message (i.e. the sequence of signs) generated by a source, the more information is being transmitted. Information then is described in terms of the statistical rarity of signs, and their combinations, produced by a source. The recipient is assumed to be aware of the relative probability of occurrence of each sign, and of combinations of signs; the information simply directs the recipient to select one of these combinations—the selection process again. Note that by allowing for a prior knowledge of the probability of combinations, the theory includes an important characteristic of practical languages: redundancy. Redundancy, that is superfluousness, does not add to information, in this sense. It helps, however, in the detection and correction of errors which may occur during the transmission of the message.

Messages are transmitted by superimposing the signs on some form of physical medium—a carrier. The carrier may be paper, electromagnetic waves, magnetic tape, etc. Every carrier has associated with it a (theoretically) quantifiable limit of the amount of signs it can accommodate per unit space or unit time, and also of the amount of distortion it is likely to introduce into messages. Information theory tells us how to estimate these limits and, more importantly, how to represent (encode) messages so that when they are transmitted via a given carrier, the decoded message contains a minimum of errors.

By guiding telecommunication engineers towards achieving the accurate transmission of messages, information theory remains to this day a corner-stone of engineering practice. But, of course, accurate transmission of inaccurate information does not make that information any 'better'. The communication engineer does not, as a rule, concern himself with the content, or 'quality', of the information. The words 'better' and 'quality' reintroduce the element of subjective judgment into our notion of information, which we again consider to be the *combination of content and representation*. So let us look at some of the factors which may affect the quality of information in this wider sense.

The quality of information

We all expect information to be *reliable* and *accurate*. In other words, information should be in agreement with reality. The trustworthiness of information is increased if it can be *verified*, that is, corroborated by independent means. Information must be sufficiently *up-to-date* for the purpose that it is to be used. It must be *complete* and *precise*, allowing the recipient to select specific details according to need. If incomplete, the degree of uncertainty must be indicated, or else it should follow some well-recognized convention. For example, the statement 'It is sunny' is conventionally taken to mean that it is sunny at the time and the place where the statement is being made. Information must be *intelligible*, that is, comprehensible by the recipient. Again, there are rules, conventions and assumptions (of language, or symbols, etc.) which when obeyed ensure this aspect of the quality of information. These general characteristics of high-quality information may not be present in practical instances.

Low-quality information can be downright *misleading* or *distorted* (as a result of the deliberate action of the source, or of the transmission process). It may be *inconsistent* with other information. It may be poorly presented, or even *incomprehensible* to the recipient. A noteworthy point here is that many products of information technology are aimed at detecting and, if possible, improving low-quality information before it reaches the recipient.

In addition to the general characteristics of high-quality information (such as one would expect from a public broadcasting or news service), there are certain desirable features associated with specific uses of information. For example, when a response is given to a well-specified inquiry, it should be *relevant* and *timely*; it should be in a form which is *conveniently handled* (interpreted, classified, stored, retrieved, updated, etc.) by the recipient; it should be of the appropriate *level of detail* and, if necessary, adequately *protected* (e.g. coded or the access to it controlled). People also appreciate if information is presented in an interesting and friendly way.

The above list is not intended to be comprehensive or uncontroversial. Its role is to encourage the reader to reconsider his or her views on what requirements to impose on existing and future products of information technology. If the quality of information is a controversial subject, a discussion of the value of information can lead into even more uncharted territory. However, this should not deter us from trying to identify some of the landmarks.

The value of information

In a recent study, branch managers of a bank were asked to rank four features affecting the quality of information made available to them (Neumann and Segev, 'A case study of user evaluation of information characteristics for systems improvement', *Information and Management*, 1979, p. 271). The four were: accuracy, content (the breadth or scope), recency (up-to-dateness) and frequency of presentation. The clear winner was content, with accuracy second.

On a more general level it has been stated (Gabor, *Lectures on Communication Theory*, MIT Press, 1951) that what people are prepared to pay money for is *exclusive* information and/or *predictive* information, the first being information tailored to the needs of the recipient, and the second enabling the recipient to select a particular action out of a whole range of possible actions. We can add to this that the perceived value of predictive information relates to the subjective value of the outcome of the selected action. For example, information on train departure times becomes the more 'valuable' the more crucial is the purpose of the journey. Thus, the value of information is not an inherent or constant quality. It depends on the needs of the recipient and on the use to which it is put.

In the most general sense, information is valued for its *organizing power*. High-quality information enables the recipient to make sense of the environment and to take action necessary to cope with changing circumstances. This power of information is rooted in the way it can represent physical and mental constructs, and is reflected by the dictionary definitions of the verb 'to inform': 'to arrange, to shape, to compose', and also 'to form (the mind, character, etc.) especially by imparting learning or instruction' (*Oxford English Dictionary*).

A possibly helpful analogy here is to think of information as the building material for a personal or a collective model of the world. Any new piece of information contributes either to the overall structure of the model, or to its utilization and testing. If, in addition, this new piece of information provides an important missing piece of the mental 'jigsaw' or helps to restructure it, we tend to attach greater value to it. To the extent that the model of the environment is internal to a person, the value of information is subjective. But for organizations, where the collective model involves transactions, data, rules, procedures, etc., it may be possible to make an objective comparison between the value of acquiring some piece of information and the cost associated with the acquisition process.

The cost of information

The cost of information is attributable to two main components: the intellectual labour involved in originating and handling it, and the non-human element made up by processing and storage equipment, distribution media, etc. The non-human costs are usually easier to quantify: it takes a certain amount of *energy* to form and transmit a representation of information, be it the spoken or written word, broadcast transmission, etc. If some physical record of the information is required, it also takes a certain amount of *material* to act as the carrier. Thus, a book, a magnetic tape or a filing card, for example, would have some inherent cost, quite apart from the production cost of the information which it carries. The equipment used in these tasks is priced on the open market.

When information is replicated in large volumes and is recorded on some physical medium, as would be the case with newspapers, books, records etc., the cost of the medium may well dominate the unit cost of the information-plus-medium. In such a case, the total product becomes a commodity, in the economic sense of that word. Thus, it can be bought and sold, and when exchanging hands, its ownership is clearly attributable.

The same is not true for 'pure' information. The originator of the information retains it, often together with legal rights to it, while also making it available to others. This fact, as well as the subjective nature of information, make it very difficult to treat it as a product or commodity. As a result, laws which attempt to treat information as an economic good—patent, trade secret, copyright or privacy laws, for instance—run into continuing problems of interpretation and enforcement. Partly to avoid these problems, 'pure' information is often given away virtually free irrespective of its cost (public information). At the other extreme, when the information has 'exclusivity value', the supplier is prepared to incur extra costs in protecting it for some time in the expectation of a high selling price (specialist reports, conferences, personalized advisory services, etc.).

Summary

Information technology has its origins in the technologies related to a restricted view of information: the generation, processing and distribution of representations of information. Examples are telecommunication and computer engineering, the data processing and office machinery industries. The products of these industries still form the bulk of information technology products. Progress in recent years has been towards the extension of this 'data engineering', or *telematics*, to an increasing range of areas of application. This has brought with it an active interest in the human aspects of information (its quality, value, utilization, etc.) or *informatics*. The new emphasis is reflected in, for example, a definition of information technology put forward in a recent US report:

> Information technology means the collection, storage, processing, dissemination and use of information. It is not confined to hardware and software, but acknowledges the importance of man and the goals he sets for this technology, the values employed in making these choices, the assessment criteria used to decide whether he is controlling the technology and is being enriched by it.

(Quoted in *Information Technology Serving Society*, edited by Chartrand and Morentz, Pergamon, 1979, p. 121.)

A similar definition is favoured by the British Advisory Council for Applied Research and Development (*Report on Information Technology*, HM Stationery Office, 1980):

> The scientific, technological and engineering disciplines and the management techniques used in information handling and processing; their applications; computers and their interaction with men and machines; and associated social, economic and cultural matters.

With these views of information technology in mind, let us look next at its uses and applications in various fields of human endeavour.

2 Information technology in action

Information technology is advancing in two main directions: first, in the development of *products* (devices, systems) and *concepts* (ideas, procedures) which have a wide range of applicability wherever people deal with information; second, in the *application* of these products and concepts to specific areas of human activity. This chapter is about the second of these directions; it outlines information technology developments in the context of occupational and marketing areas, such as the office or the home. The emphasis here is on how the products and concepts appear to the users and what sort of changes they imply to existing ways of dealing with information. In the process, some of the emerging products and concepts believed to be of particular significance will be identified. A more detailed description of the products and of the concepts behind them will be taken up in subsequent chapters. One word of warning before starting: products, concepts, applications of information technology are currently in a state of rapid evolution. Sometimes it is very difficult to determine the stage of development of a particular product or idea from the published details. But for would-be users it is vital to know whether some new offering is

(a) what is already in routine use;
(b) what has just been introduced, or
(c) what is about to be introduced;
(d) what is currently in the research and development stage; and
(e) what someone thinks is technically possible.

In the descriptions that follow, distinctions will be made between what exists and what is possible, in terms of the state-of-the-art at the beginning of the 1980s.

The range of applications of information technology is as wide as the range of activities where information is used. In terms of the number of jobs affected by it, the amount of effort, publicity and capital invested, however, one field stands out as the most significant area of work: the office. For example, it has been estimated by the US Department of Labor, that by 1985 over 50 million people will be working in American offices, and about a million million dollars will be spent as direct office costs. So this is where we start our look at information technology in action. Following that, we shall turn to some other occupational areas listed in Table 1.1: the manufacturing industries, commercial, financial and communication services, health care, education and training, and finally to where we are all involved—the home.

The office

Information technology made itself felt in the office much before the present push towards an 'electronic office'. The products of information technology in widespread use (group (a) on the scale of developments given above) include typewriters (manual and electric), telephones, telex, dictating machines, microfilm readers, calculators, reprographic (copying) equipment, facsimile and automatic addressing machines, paging systems, in-house exchanges, to name just the most important products. Figure 2.1 shows the value of sales of such equipment in western Europe in 1978.

Fig. 2.1 Value of sales of information technology equipment in Western Europe in 1978. (Source: *Economist*, 18 November 1978, p. 127)

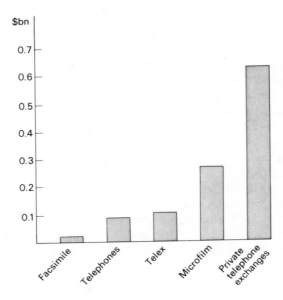

In spite of their diversity, these items in the 'office of the present' have a number of features in common:

(a) They serve as technical aids to some frequently repeated operations in the office.
(b) They largely rely on mechanical or electromechanical principles for their operation, and are, as a result, slower than what could be achieved by using electronic equivalents.
(c) They are essentially simple to operate.
(d) Many are largely self-contained, non-interconnected pieces of equipment (with the exception, of course, of telecommunication systems—telephone, telex and facsimile).

A new information technology of the 'office of the future' aims to cope with the information handling problems of the office at two distinct levels. First, by offering a new, electronic medium to supplement or, where appropriate, to replace more traditional media such as paper, together with equipment related to the use of traditional media, such as filing cabinets. Second, by taking a fresh look at the tasks performed in the office, with the view to *integrating* (combining) some of the functions and *automating* some of the tasks.

These two levels will be examined in turn, starting with the 'electronic office', which uses electronic means of dealing with some of the established office functions. At the present time, the main currencies of office activity are documents, visual presentations and spoken words.

Document preparation

Documents may include a text and a graphical (diagrammatic) component. In the 'office of the present', a document is usually produced by several people: someone, say an administrator or manager, who originates and checks it, a typist, who prepares the text, and a draughtsman or artist who prepares the diagrams. The most highly mechanized stage of the document preparation process is text preparation, aided currently by the typewriter. The completely mechanical typewriter, invented about 1714, first gave way to its electric (strictly speaking, electromechanical) and electronic counterparts, and more recently to the so-called *word processor*. (In the view of the author, 'word processor' is something of a misnomer since such machines deal with only one aspect of words—their written form. A more appropriate name would be *text processor*, which would release the term 'word processor' for equipment which is able to handle words in both their written and spoken forms.)

The major step in the transition from the office typewriter to the text processor was the conversion of the keyboard mechanism to the generation of not only printed images of characters but also of a *standard digital character code* uniquely corresponding to each character. With the text in computer-compatible form, it becomes possible to store and manipulate it in various ways before reconverting it to printed form, using established computer methods. It is worth noting here that the digitally coded form of characters making up text can also be generated by means other than keyboards. One method, which has yet to reach routine acceptance, is the conversion of already printed text and of handwritten text directly into digital form by means of *character recognition equipment* (see p. 82). Such equipment currently does not offer a 100 per cent success rate, with handwriting posing the greater problems for the equipment designer. Even further down the development scale is equipment for the direct conversion of spoken words into digitally represented text (see p. 101).

Text preparation in the 'electronic office' is aided by electronic keyboards linked to a computer (processor and memory), a video screen and a printer. The typist does not handle paper, instead the text appears on the screen. As far as the typist is concerned, the text is created and manipulated there and, when completed, sent away for storage, printing or even photo-typesetting. When creating the screen-image of text, the computer usually presents a set of pre-programmed formats as options (e.g. A4 blank or letterhead, memo blank or letterhead, etc.). The margins and tab positions are set automatically according to the option chosen. A cursor (a small rectangle of light) is used to indicate on the screen where the next keyed character will be positioned. Cursor-control keys allow this position to be changed at will, and, of course, the cursor moves on after each key-stroke.

Automatic formatting facilities usually available on such equipment include justification, hyphenation, headings, footnotes, tabulation and change of typeface by few key-strokes. Text manipulation facilities include the insertion, deletion or replacement of a single letter or passages of text, the replacement of a specific word in all its occurrences by another word, the pulling in of prepared passages, the ability to locate specific words or reference numbers anywhere in the text, and, in some cases, even spelling correction.

Diagrams and other graphical material can be incorporated into digitally manipulated text either as a separate operation at the final printing stage, or by creating the images directly in digital form and manipulating them as part of the total representation. In the former case, the layout of the text is adjusted to leave room for the graphics, but the lettering, captions, signs, etc., may be produced at the same time as the rest of the text. In the latter case, special *graphical input devices* or direct computer commands are used to create and modify (edit) images on the display screen.

Document-processing machines can be either stand-alone or communicating, as shown in Fig. 2.2(a), (b). A stand-alone machine has

Fig. 2.2 Text processor configurations:

(a) A stand-alone text processor consists of a terminal containing a processor, keyboard and display unit, and is linked to a memory device and printer

(b) Communicating text processors can gain access to common memory and printing devices via a switching unit

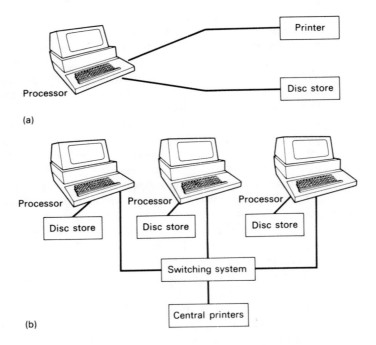

built into it all the facilities needed to key in, store or modify text. The printing of the final document may be either part of these local facilities, or it may be done with a shared-resource machine, on a more expensive centralized printer which accepts some electronically stored version of text to produce a high-quality printed document. Communicating machines are able to shunt around electronically coded text and graphics from one machine to another, along in-house telecommunication lines (so-called *local networks*—see p. 111). In addition, shared-logic machines can also link to a central (usually in-house) computer installation which may be much better at processing, storing and printing than stand-alone machines.

Due to the higher cost, however, of the central installation, its power is shared among the several work-stations which link to it (hence the name shared-logic or shared-processor). Text processing, combined with communication at a distance, can be used when office personnel are not located at the same site. For example, a development which has been tried on an experimental basis in the United States enables an executive to record dictation on a dictating machine in his office or home, and to replay those tapes automatically into another machine over the telephone. The second machine may be in the home of a typist who prefers not to travel to the office. The typist prepares the documentation using a text processor and transmits it in digital form, again over the telephone, to the company's headquarters. There the document is checked for accuracy and then printed on headed paper.

Current experience with document preparation suggests that electronic methods are cost-effective only when a document is a long report or manual, or when use can be made of previously created text, or else when the text processors are in continuous use, for example, in a typing pool. Intangible considerations include the visual appearance of the finished document, the turn-round time in its preparation and the fact that text has been 'captured', that is converted to computer-compatible form.

The preparation of one particular type of document, the internal memo, is by implication not a cost-effective use of a text processor. Instead, memos can be sent through *computer-based message systems* (see p. 118). Such systems are being introduced by some large organizations. The input to such systems is usually of the same form as that to text processors (keyboard or character-recognition equipment). What is more unusual is the way the messages are distributed and presented to the addressee. So let us look at them, and at some other new office facilities, as means of document distribution.

Document distribution

Documents in the electronic office may be distributed either as electronically coded images presented on a display device (with the options of recording them as data for future reference and re-display), or as computer print-outs for filing in a conventional filing system, or as computer-produced *microfilm* (see pp. 81 and 96). The distribution of documents on paper is aided by the recent generation of fast, high-quality printers. These include laser printers and photo-typesetters, as well as refinements of the more conventional printing methods such as ink-jet printers, electrostatic and xerographic printers. A common characteristic of the new generation of printing devices is that they can reproduce text faster than the typist's typing speed, so they offer the opportunity of separating the text production process from copy production, both in space and time.

Electronic methods of document distribution are based on the same principle as document preparation: the ability to represent text by computer-compatible signals. Just as these signals can be processed within the computer to yield the formatting and editing features described earlier, they can also be transmitted at the speed of light. The most well-established of the electronic methods make use of *telex and facsimile transmission* (see pp. 117 and 118). The national and international telex networks already provide a means of getting text from person-to-person with acknowledgement of receipt and storage of the messages. More recent developments aim at replacing the telex terminal with a text processor. This new generation of faster, silent enhanced-telex terminals will form the gateways to a computerized *teletex* network (see p. 117). Once international standards for this are agreed, an A4-size page can be transmitted automatically in about 10 s. Optionally, the messages can be held centrally until the cheap-rate transmission rates start—the so-called *store-and-forward* method of transmission (see p. 118).

Facsimile methods for the remote copying of pages of documents have been in existence for over 100 years (see p. 118). They can cope with graphics as well as text material in their original form, that is, by transmitting an exact copy. At present, an A4 page can be transmitted in about 3 min, at a resolution of about 38 lines/cm. Using improved coding methods and digital signals, these can be improved by a factor of two or three, still using the telephone or telex networks. However, if satellite or broadcast microwave links are employed, transmission rates of several hundred pages per minute become possible. Again, international standards are yet to be agreed for these faster, high-resolution facsimile services. These improved telex and facsimile services are expected to become widely available to businesses in the mid-1980s.

Historically more recent than telex and facsimile are computer-based document transmission methods. These enable people to send and receive messages, such as memos, reports, reminders, via a network of interconnected computer terminals. (These terminals may be the text-processing work-stations mentioned earlier.) The terminals may be linked via an in-house wired or wireless *local network* (e.g. telephone lines or microwave links—see p. 111), or the national and international telecommunication networks. In addition to document transmission, a computer-based message network offers the possibility of *computer conferencing*. In a computer conference, a discussion document (or a nominated topic) is commented upon by participants at various locations, over a period of time. The contributions are usually stored in the sequence of their entry into the system.

In a computer-based system, messages are created in just the same way as in a text processor. But being based on larger, more powerful computers, the systems usually allow data held in the computer's memory (e.g., standard paragraphs, tables of figures) to be incorporated into the text of the message. A message can be addressed to an individual or to a group. The system incorporates safeguards to preserve the necessary confidentiality of messages, their integrity (accuracy) during storage, transmission and reproduction. The recipient is informed by the computer of a waiting message as soon as he or she contacts the system.

The messages can then be read, either in their entirety or just to identify the sender and possibly the first line of the message. The computer can arrange messages in a stated order of priority. The message then can be deleted, read again on the screen, filed electronically, printed out as a hard copy, or sent to a third party without the need to re-enter it.

A very interesting feature of some such systems is that messages can be initiated by the computer itself, in response to some earlier stated requirement. For example, the computer may contain the dates of meetings in its memory, or a list of new documents or books, etc. circulating in the office, and notify individuals about items of particular interest to them.

Computer-based message systems are currently tailor-made to the requirements of specific organizations, and are operated by them for their own purposes. However, public services, similar to teletex, are also in the pipeline. While teletex is essentially a transmission facility, *videotex* (such as Britain's Prestel) allows the storage of text, etc. in a network of computers (see p. 125).

Document storage and retrieval

It has been recently estimated (Haider, in *Office Automation*, Infotech, 1980) that there is the equivalent of 20 million million pages of A4 paper stored in offices in the USA, and this is growing at a rate of 1 million pages every minute of every day. Apart from the physical problem of storage, this presents an increasingly difficult organizational problem in locating documents relevant to specific topics. It has been estimated that, in the USA, an office professional spends about 20–30 per cent of his or her time just looking for information. The computer-based distribution systems, with the added facility of storage of computer-coded text, offer one approach to reducing the physical size of records, and to mechanizing their search and retrieval. The records, unfortunately, first have to be converted into computer-compatible form, and can be consulted only after reconversion via some printing or display device.

There is also another important disadvantage to current methods of computer-held documentation: diagrams are profligate in the use of computer memory. So documents with graphical content are best adapted to the 'electronic office' by alternative means: *video discs* (see p. 70) or *microforms* (microfilm or microfiche—see p. 95).

Microforms are estimated to reduce the storage space requirements, in comparison with paper, by 98 per cent (see p. 98). They can be generated either by photographic reduction of documents or by direct output from computers. In the latter case, text created on the video screen can be recorded on film by means of a computer-output microform (com) recorder. Microforms can be read by means of optically magnifying reading devices, or by equipment which presents the magnified image on a video display.

Recently, microform technology has been combined with computerized indexing and retrieval techniques. The result is a device able to hold several million frames, and locate and present any one of these, in response to a keyword request, in a matter of seconds. On the screen, the microfilmed information can be combined with up-to-date text or graphics, and if necessary, the resulting image re-recorded for future reference.

Visual presentations

We have already noted the central position of video screen in the 'electronic office'. It is used in the preparation and presentation of textual material and, in some systems, of pictures stored in computer memory or as microforms. It also gives access of visual information held in data sources outside the organization itself. The preparation of graphical material is aided by computer programs and also by special-purpose computer graphic devices. These enable people to set up bar-charts, line drawings, block diagrams and other standard office presentations with only a few instructions, and without special training. They also accept hand-drawn images, handwriting or already existing photographic or television images, convert them to computer-compatible form and store or transmit them. Again, the key operation here is the conversion of information (pictorial information in this case) to a coded form which can be manipulated by digital methods.

An interesting by-product of this approach is that the code so generated can be transmitted to remote locations by a variety of means. If the picture is steady or slowly changing it can be transmitted along telephone lines or by broadcast (slow-scan tv). Rapidly changing pictures require television-quality wiring or broadcast links for their transmission. Such links may be internal to an organization or can utilize public telecommunication facilities (e.g. satellites or cables).

Spoken words

The telephone is, and will remain for the foreseeable future, the main office technology for dealing with spoken words. There are many advances and improvements to the basic telephone service. These are reviewed on p. 34. Most of these stem from the application of computer technology in the telephone itself, in the exchanges (private and public) and in the representation of speech by computer-compatible signals. Some of these advances are aimed at overcoming the problems that have led, in the past, to the failure of an estimated two calls in three when the called party was engaged or away from the telephone. These problems are also being addressed by other, computer-based equipment. This can store speech until it is ready to be received. For example, 'vocal memos' can be sent to any extension on an internal telephone network, or in combination with electronic mail, a written report with a spoken commentary can be prepared.

From an office point of view, for example, it is becoming possible to interlink a number of telephones into a *telephone conference* (see p. 60). The participants in the conference can be reached by telephone. Prior to the meeting they may have already received, by electronic mail, the documentation to be used during the meeting. By using a graphical input device connected to the telephone line, they can draw diagrams which are seen instantaneously by all the participants on video display units, also connected to the telephone.

Dictating machines and automatic answering machines are also widely used aids in offices. They, and the people who use them, are unlikely to be displaced in the near future by automated speech typewriters or speech input–output computers, since the automatic recognition of speech is still at the laboratory stage (see Chapter 12).

Working in the electronic office

Before moving on to look at what may be in store for the 'office of the future' in the longer term, let us pause to consider some of the effects of the 'electronic office' on people who work with the new equipment. Perhaps the most striking point about the 'electronic office' is that it is not significantly different from the conventional office. The emphasis of the new technology so far has been on enhancing existing equipment or on offering an alternative medium to paper. It has not, so far, aimed at automating complete jobs, rather at making them faster and more convenient to perform.

Whether this aim has been achieved, and whether it has contributed significantly to the overall efficiency of the office are difficult to gauge. It has been estimated that in document preparation up to 70 per cent savings can be made if the author changes from the long-hand method of composition to the dictating machine and if the typist can make up the document from pre-stored passages. The electronic filing and retrieving of documents combined with an efficient indexing and keywording facility are also claimed to save secretarial and executive time (once people become familiar with the equipment, and once the equipment is functioning reliably). What is clear is that in offices where the new electronic equipment has been introduced people had to get used to new machines and new work patterns. For example, text processors are more cost-effective if they are used virtually continuously. Organizationally, this often means the creation of a 'word-processing centre', akin to a typing pool. For the typists, the change meant having to undergo a period of training (in some cases, all too short and inadequate training), then having to operate a machine which has no need for traditional layout skills but requires continuous concentration. As a result, some text-processor operators feel socially isolated (*Office Automation*, Infotech, Series 8, No. 3, 1980). A study by the Cambridge-based Applied Psychology Unit of the Medical Research Council has reported that some users of computerized office equipment are intimidated by the machines, feel inadequate in understanding what goes on 'behind the screen', and perceive such systems as 'unnecessary alien intruders' in the office. The need for adequate training and for a gradual, well-justified introduction of new equipment is evident from all reports published on the impact of the 'electronic office'.

The integrated office

A significant drawback of the 'office of the present' is that the various pieces of equipment used there are rarely compatible with one another.

Text, graphic and voice-processing machines are not standardized, and output from one cannot be easily utilized as input to another.

Standardization is one answer to this problem, and it is happening on a limited scale. Its opponents claim, however, that the technology is evolving so rapidly that standards would stifle the innovator. The other approach is the introduction of local (in-house) communication networks which allow the interlinking of all kinds of electronic equipment. An example of such a network is shown in Fig. 13.3 (p. 111).

Inside a building, the network takes the form of cables. Between offices the connection may be based on telephone lines, or microwave or light links. The idea of a local network is similar to the electrical outlets in a house, to which different individually incompatible pieces of equipment may be connected. The difference, though, is in the purpose of the connection: for the local network it is the interchange of data. The transmission rates in the network are high—up to a million characters a second (at these rates it would take about 20 s to transmit the entire text of the Bible).

Once installed, the local office network has the potential for substituting the flow of computer-coded information for the flow of paper. It can interconnect text processors, personal computers and terminals to high-quality printers, computer-based file stores, facsimile machines and other electronic office equipment.

The sort of job that could be speeded up through the use of a local network is the preparation of an urgent report. An 'electronic memo' asking key contributors to comment on an appended draft report can be sent by electronic mail. The draft can contain statistical and graphical information from a computer-file store. The received comments can be incorporated into the final draft through a combination of electronic mail and text processing. When the report is in an acceptable form, a high-quality copy can be printed and, if necessary, transmitted by facsimile to remote sites.

An important feature of the local network concept is the possibility of interconnection with other company-wide, national or international data networks through a computer 'gateway' also linked to the ring.

An alternative approach to the 'integrated office' is to incorporate what are currently separate pieces of office equipment into a 'multi-function work station'. Although this concept is in its early stages of development, it appears to aim at the complete replacement of the desk, the telephone, the office typewriter and the filing cabinet by a single electronic box having visual and voice links with the user. The visual display initially shows representations of the various items of office equipment, such as the filing cabinet. The user 'opens the cabinet' by means of an electronic pointing device, and has its contents displayed as a catalogue. A particular document can then be selected, its contents electronically modified, if necessary, and printed by simply pointing to the representation of the printer on the screen.

However, these are early days for the 'office of the future'. For one thing, it is by no means clear that the office, in the sense of a centralized administrative organization, will survive in the long term. But even in the nearer term, the cost-effective use of the 'new technology' requires the re-thinking of the entire pattern of flow of information within the office and the re-training of staff. This, in turn, is likely to demand organizational changes whose effects are bound to be even more far-reaching than the piece-meal introduction of the 'electronic office'.

Manufacturing industries

Manufacturing industries are among the earliest and most well-established fields of application of information technology. Computers, in particular, have come to play a role in keeping management informed about the state of production, orders, stocks, finances, personnel and so on, as part of *management information systems* (see p. 121). They also became tools for production planning, product design and industrial research. And, just as importantly, they have assumed an increasingly pervasive role in the control of production processes and manufacturing equipment, in other words, in industrial automation.

At first, in the sixties and early seventies, these three areas—management, design and production—were looked at as separate activities, as far as computer applications were concerned. They were catered for by computer systems of different complexity and cost. More recently, the emergence of more sophisticated and cheaper computers, and communication links has created an opportunity to:

(a) interlink (integrate) the separate computer systems of a company, so that information can be collected, handled and distributed more rapidly and conveniently, by means of a *distributed data-base system*;
(b) incorporate microcomputers and other information technology products directly into the manufactured product.

As examples of these developments, we shall look briefly at two industries: publishing and printing, and car manufacture.

Publishing and printing

The publishing and printing industries are in the business of mass production and distribution of information, in the form of books, periodicals, newspapers and other printed matter. Their production cycle involves the entire range of operations which are of concern to information technology: the generation (authoring), processing (editing), storage (printing and warehousing), dissemination (marketing) and use (management) of information. As a direct consequence, their activities are among the first to be directly affected by advances in information technology. In publishing, the main innovation is *electronic publishing*. The essence of this is the replacement of the traditional means of printing, storage and dissemination of paper by the equivalent operations on electronic messages.

In electronic publishing, the text may be prepared on a computer-based text processor. Some publishers already provide their authors with text processors and so reduce the time taken for editing the manuscript. The use of a text processor also allows the rapid production of camera-ready copy. Advanced text processors incorporate various authoring aids. One system, developed at the Bell Laboratories, in the USA, includes a feature for simplifying an author's convoluted prose. For example, the following extract from Lincoln's Gettysburg address was typed into the text processor: 'Four score and seven years ago our fathers brought forth on this continent a new nation conceived in Liberty, and dedicated to the proposition that all men are created equal.' The processor converted this into: 'Eighty-seven years ago our grandfathers created a free nation here. They based it on the idea that everybody is created equal.' The author, of course, is not bound to accept the processor's recommendation, but it might serve as a welcome 'second opinion'.

An alternative to printing the text so prepared is to use a form of 'electronic mail', since the text is now held and distributed as computerized data. Would-be users must have at their disposal a *visual display terminal* (also called a vdu—visual display unit), which informs them about the range of available 'publications' and allows them to select specific items, either for viewing on the screen, or storing for later reference in electronic form or printing on a local printing device.

Perhaps the first commercial form of electronic publishing is *videotex* (see p. 125). The Prestel system in Britain places at the disposal of information providers a means of reaching a nationwide audience—indeed, a world-wide one—through the telephone network. If a telephone subscriber also has available to him or her a specially modified television receiver (or some other suitable computer terminal), this opens the way to a storehouse of diverse information (news, reference, advertising, advisory and other material). The user can select from this range by pressing keys on a keyboard in accordance with instructions displayed on the screen of the receiver. The information provider can set a price for each screenful of information. The user's bill is then dependent on the specific 'frames' of information requested, and also on the time for which the receiver has been connected to the computer store.

Although Prestel was the first public videotex system, other systems of this type are being introduced in several countries, including France, Canada, West Germany, the Netherlands, the United States, and others. Many of these differ from Prestel, and each other, in terms of detailed features and, at present, lack of technical compatibility.

A somewhat different electronic publishing medium, *teletext* (not to be confused with teletex), uses the television, instead of the telephone, as the distribution network for computer-coded text and pictures (see p. 126). As with videotex, the information provider uses the text processing and data storing facilities of the computer to prepare and hold the material. But the next step in getting this material to the recipient is where teletext differs significantly from videotex: the recipient of teletext does not normally have any means of contacting the computer data-store directly to ask for a specific publication. This is because broadcast transmission (e.g. television) is normally from (a set of) central transmitters to millions of receivers but not the other way around. With the telephone system, and therefore with videotex, the user has a direct, two-way connection to the computer data-store. As a consequence, videotex provides a faster, more controllable access for the user than teletext. Even though teletext provides some selection facilities from the total information being transmitted, the techniques currently used severely restrict the amount of information which can be so transmitted. The economics of the two systems are also different: with teletext the publisher has, at the present time, no means of knowing who has been viewing the published material, since all the user requires to see this material is a modified television receiver. The inability of publishers to raise revenue from users of teletext has so far restricted its commercial exploitation as a publishing medium.

In addition to the electronic publishing media (the combination of computer, telecommunication and display technologies), progress is being made with the use of two other media for publishing: *microforms* (see p. 95) and *video tape and disc* (see p. 67).

Microform technology currently enables the publisher to reproduce 200 pages on a so-called *ultra-fiche*, and video discs can hold over 50 000 still frames (text or pictures or both). Of particular interest is the combination of these two media with computer technology: the computer can be used to prepare and edit the material; it can produce a direct output on microfilm; it can aid the user to find a specific item in a library of microfilms; it can control the replay of video discs so that a particular frame is found and displayed, wherever it is on the disc, in less than a second.

These new publishing media offer some significant advantages over the conventional methods: the production time is reduced, changes and 'new editions' are more conveniently made, the distributed medium (electronic signal, microfilm, disc) may be cheaper than a bound volume of print. Against this, however, the cost to the end user is currently a great deal higher, because special display devices are needed in each case. These 'reading devices' are also less convenient to handle and read than print on paper. But these are exactly the same problems which are being experienced in the office and other applications of information technology and we can expect a concentrated research effort to solve them. In the meanwhile, electronic information technology is making inroads into the conventional printing side of book and newspaper publication.

The first major challenge to the established techniques of letterpress and lithography came in the late 1960s: it was *photo-typesetting*. Figure 2.3 compares the stages of preparing a printed page by the three methods. The computer helps in the editing of the manuscript and eliminates the need for molten-lead typesetting machines. More recently, the computer has also been employed to assemble ('make-up') a printed page from its various components—the galleys of text, graphics, advertisements, etc. It allows experimentation with the layout, choice of typeface, etc., on a video display before finalizing each page. The next step is likely to be the introduction of complete text and picture-processing facilities into the process, where the entire contents of a publication are held and manipulated as computer data. This development can then link directly with yet another separately developing area—the electronic transmission of made-up pages for printing at a remote location (see p. 118). The international edition of the *Herald Tribune*, for example, is now published simultaneously in London, Paris, Zurich and Hong Kong by transmitting *facsimiles* of each page. The Hong Kong copy is sent via a

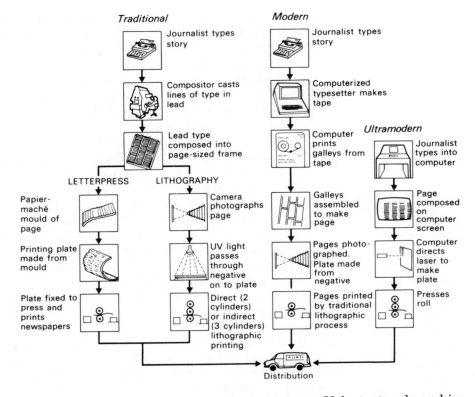

Fig. 2.3 The three ages of printing technology. (After *Economist*, 19 July 1980, p. 99)

Traditional

Journalist types story

Compositor casts lines of type in lead

Lead type composed into page-sized frame

LETTERPRESS

Papier-maché mould of page

Printing plate made from mould

Plate fixed to press and prints newspapers

LITHOGRAPHY

Camera photographs page

UV light passes through negative on to plate

Direct (2 cylinders) or indirect (3 cylinders) lithographic printing

Modern

Journalist types story

Computerized typesetter makes tape

Computer prints galleys from tape

Galleys assembled to make page

Pages photographed. Plate made from negative

Pages printed by traditional lithographic process

Ultramodern

Journalist types into computer

Page composed on computer screen

Computer directs laser to make plate

Presses roll

Distribution

satellite, the process taking about 5–10 min/page. If the text and graphics were handled completely as computer data, the facsimile stage could be by-passed and transmission speeded up. Graphics, however, currently present a major stumbling block to the computer since the amount of detail in them makes their storage and transmission complex and expensive.

The range of new technologies available to the printing and publishing industries keeps increasing rapidly. However, the cost is high, the implications of change for publishers, printers and the public are great. In an industry where some publishers are yet to make the change from letterpress to lithography, any radical moves will be motivated only by the economic unviability of existing methods. With the increasing cost of paper and printing ink, of sophisticated printing machines, of distribution and marketing, the replacement of many centrally-produced paper publications by electronically distributed, stored and displayed data, with an optional, locally produced printed version, looks a definite future possibility.

Car manufacture

The design, production, driving, servicing and sale of cars and trucks involves a great many operations on information. These include collection of data to aid the planning of a new product, the detailed decisions about its design, the preparation of instructions on the manufacture and assembly of component parts, collection of test data, etc.

At the present time, most car manufacturers use computers to assist with the design stage (computer-aided design) and for overall management control of the production process. Computers are also used to automate some of the manufacturing functions (e.g. computer-controlled welding, painting, assembly devices, the so-called 'shop-floor robots') and to keep track of components and spares in the warehouse. As a rule, these tend to be separate computer systems.

To improve the flow of information, the individual computers can be linked together through a *local network* (see p. 111). In one major UK truck plant, the network links seven computers and about 200 terminals. The terminals on the shop floor may be used to check the stock position of a component and to order parts from the warehouse. The warehouse itself is completely automated. A truck may be made up of several thousand parts, and these kept in tens of thousands of different storage locations. The parts are located and moved by microcomputer-controlled cranes, acting on instructions from the shop-floor terminals. The results of tests on the completed trucks are also entered into the computer network. In this way, information is available not only on the performance of each truck, but also on any defects (these can be analysed automatically for patterns of faults), and on the current state of the production. On the basis of the warehousing and production-line information, the terminals in the management offices can be used for a fine control of the parts ordering and holding, and even to check on the number of people who may be absent from work on a particular day. This manufacturer is also using a local network for production-flow monitoring in one of its car plants, and a private *videotex* system for sales support (see p. 125).

Another European manufacturer has been for some time using a system which enables its dealers to order spare parts from a central depot by keying its identification details on a keyboard which is linked to the warehouse computer through the public telephone network. The computer acknowledges the order and informs the dealer about availability by a 'spoken' message. Such *voice response* systems (see p. 101) are now commercially available and are used in many industrial situations where the recipient of information does not require a visible or printed response, or where the visual information needs constant attention and the sound output is an additional form of communication.

The need for an additional channel of communication also arises in supplying information to the driver of a car or truck, who is concentrating on the immediate road conditions. Computer-produced audible warnings can be currently produced to inform the driver about abnormal conditions detected by sensors mounted in the vehicle. Alternatively, the driver may be warned about road conditions further ahead by means of broadcast traffic information. In a system in use in Germany, and a similar one undergoing tests in Britain, traffic information is superimposed on radio programs, and decoded by a microprocessor linked to the car's radio. The driver has the option of receiving traffic news only (related to a 30 km area around each of a network of transmitters), or ordinary broadcasts interrupted by traffic news, or just the uninterrupted radio programs.

For many years, radios were the only information-technology products inside a car, representing up to 0.2 per cent of its cost. Estimates are that by 1985 between 5 and 15 per cent of the cost of a car will be contributed to by electronic systems. The first confirmation of this trend came in late 1980 when the American General Motors Corporation announced that all its cars would include a microcomputer system 'about the size of a textbook'. The main functions of the system relate to improving the engine performance, giving better fuel economy and controlling exhaust emission, by regulating the air–fuel mixture, the idling speed and the spark timing. Air conditioning and seat positioning can also be controlled, with the computer storing the preferred seat position for various drivers. Diagnostic facilities built into the computer monitor the operation of various components, record all malfunctions, warn the driver about them, and even adjust the operating conditions of the engine to compensate for the fault until repairs are made. Similar systems are being developed by most major car manufacturers, with emphasis on automating the routine under-the-bonnet functions, and keeping the driver informed about factors which affect the safety and controllability of the car.

Possible longer term developments include the use of computers to respond to visual images (*computer vision*—see p. 83) and to spoken commands (*speech recognition*—see p. 101). Computer-vision systems are already being applied, in an experimental way, to aid in automatic inspection, materials handling and assembly tasks (see Fig. 2.4). When

Fig. 2.4 A model visual inspection system. It is made up of the sensing, image-processing and flaw-analysis subsystems. The part-handling subsystem acts on the outcome of the flaw analysis (© 1980 IEEE. Reprinted, with permission, from *Computer*, May 1980)

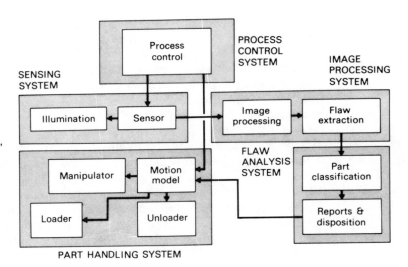

installed in cars, they could warn the driver of hazardous situations on the road. Commercial automatic speech recognition systems are at present limited to the identification of isolated words rather than of connected speech. Experimental applications to date include warehousing and sorting, preparation of instructions for 'robots', etc. Their potential lies in controlling computerized equipment by voice commands in situations where the use of keyboards is not appropriate.

If the office and manufacturing industry are good testing grounds for the potential of information technology, the field of financial transactions has been using it for some time out of sheer necessity. The reason for this is that every money transaction is also an information transaction: a record needs to be made (formally or informally) about the amount, the purpose, the parties involved, the date, etc. And the number of transactions has been rapidly increasing over the years, as indicated in Fig. 2.5. The London clearing banks handle over 2000 million cheques

Fig. 2.5 Trends in the growth of various forms of non-cash payments in Britain, projected to 1985. (Source: Inter-Bank Research Organisation)

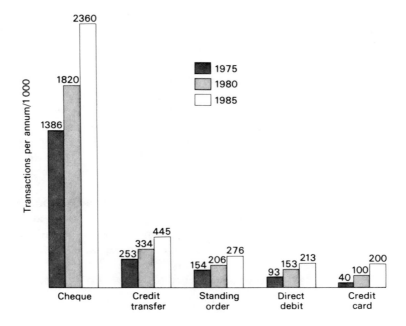

and credit transfers a year, the American banks fifteen times as many. Until relatively recently, all such transactions were recorded on paper and processed by hand or by means of slow electromechanical equipment. This has proved woefully inadequate in the face of the explosive growth of transactions, accompanied by acute shortages of clerical workers in the large cities and pressure for shorter working hours by bank staff. The technological response to this need for a faster, more efficient, less labour-intensive method of handling financial transactions has been given the name of *electronic payment services* in the UK. In the United States, it is known as *electronic funds transfer* (EFT).

There are several distinct historical stages in the progress to electronic money transactions. The first stage involved the processing by computer of accounts and payments, within and between banks. The major banks have installed their own computer networks, with terminals in the branches. The use of a standardized commercial code for identifying banks on cheques, etc., in conjunction with a standardized set of stylized symbols suitable for *optical and magnetic character recognition* (electronic shape identification), has helped to convert data about transactions to computer-compatible form. Later, it became possible to transfer such data from one bank's computer to that of another, by means of a network of leased, high-quality telephone lines. Such clearing-house operations were at first done on a national basis, but by the late seventies an international banking *data network*, Swift (Society for Worldwide Interbank Financial Telecommunications), came into operation. Initially, it linked 500 banks in more than 15 countries (see p. 116).

The second stage brought into this network the computers of some of the organizations, companies, etc., who conduct a large volume of business with the banks. Transactions like payments of salaries, share dividends, tax deductions, etc., could now be handled by the transfer of data, rather than of slips of paper. Standing orders (pre-authorized payments) and the preparation of statements could also be computerized. This stage was reached and consolidated during the seventies in the western industrialized countries.

The third stage in this process extends the range of electronic financial transactions even further, by installing banking terminals for public use. Initially, such automated terminals ('teller machines') were installed in the banks themselves, enabling people to draw cash by means of a debit card (as opposed to a credit card, to help distinguish between money that is in one's account and money being borrowed from the credit-card organization). Debit cards carry a magnetic stripe to identify the account to the terminal by means of a digital code. The user of the card has also to key in a personal identity number on the terminal's keyboard. The computer authorizes payment only if the two codes correspond and if the account will not be overdrawn as a result of the transaction.

This is the level of development reached in Britain in beginning of the 1980s. In the USA and in France, and indeed in a single experimental case in Britain, debit-card terminals are being placed in shops and other public places. In principle, the terminals could be installed anywhere people spend money. They would even circumvent the need to withdraw cash, if it is to be spent again directly at the same location. Instead, the buyer's account would be debited and the seller's account credited, by the banking network. (A behind-the-scenes transaction is involved here between the buyer's and the seller's banks.) Indeed, it is not even necessary for the transaction to be handled by a terminal connected to the banking computer network. It is technically possible to use the magnetic stripe (or some other form of electronic data storage) on the card to hold the details of the transactions for which it has been used, so that the amounts being spent are deducted from the card's nominal starting value, until that value is exhausted. At that stage, a new card could be issued. (Note the contrast with the function of the cheque, and the extra security for the seller.) The introduction of public banking terminals is coincident with another application of information technology, this time in retailing. The late 1970s saw the introduction of computer terminals at supermarket check-outs, department store counters, and other points where the sale of goods takes place. In the jargon of computer marketing, these have become known as 'point-of-sale' or *POS terminals*. There are two main types of such terminal—interconnected and free-standing.

Interconnected POS terminals are part of a network of such terminals, linked via communication lines to the retail organization's own computer system. They transmit data relating to each sale as it takes place. A free-standing terminal is a computer in its own right, which processes and stores data about the transactions. It may also exchange data with a central computer at pre-determined intervals, say at the end of a working day.

In each case, the terminals are equipped with some means of supplying data about the details of a purchase in computer-coded form, and a printer to produce a receipt for the customer. The items purchased are identified by means of a bar-code, similar to the one shown in Fig. 2.6.

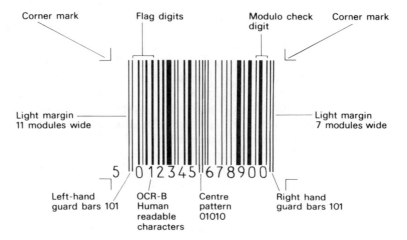

Fig. 2.6 Components of the EAN (European Article Numbering) system of bar-codes. Items for sale in a supermarket are identified by printed bar-codes which can be scanned by a laser at the check-out

Corner mark   Flag digits   Modulo check digit   Corner mark

Light margin 11 modules wide

Light margin 7 modules wide

5 0 1 2 3 4 5 6 7 8 9 0 0

Left-hand guard bars 101   OCR-B Human readable characters   Centre pattern 01010   Right hand guard bars 101

Each type of merchandise sold in a store is allocated to a unique code, printed on its wrapping. At the point of sale, the code is read by a device linked to the terminal. The computer cross-references this code with a price table stored in its memory and prints out the details on the receipt. At the same time, it records or transmits these details for up-dating the stock-list of the firm, held in the central computer. Management can then be supplied with necessary information about the current trading position, so that stock-holding can be finely controlled, and popular sales lines can be quickly spotted. An obvious possibility, not yet realized on a wide basis, is to use the same terminal to connect also to the banking network. A customer then would use a debit card to settle the bill, as noted earlier.

There are several reasons why such integration is slow to materialize in practice. The obvious one is expense. It is not clear who is going to benefit most from installing the terminals and the telecommunication lines. Also, the technology is not yet sufficiently robust to cater for the secure and reliable interconnection of different large-terminal networks. If difficulties of this type are overcome in the longer run, the way will be open to link the payments–sales system to the information network of manufacturing industry on the one hand, and to the home-shopping mail-order networks on the other. The benefits, and costs, of such a large-scale trading network can only be contemplated at this stage. Whether such a network will ever come into existence depends, of course, not only on its technical feasibility, but also on its public acceptance, economic viability (coloured by factors like the availability of raw materials, energy and the general economic climate) and the willingness of the various interests involved in such an arrangement to cooperate.

On a somewhat smaller scale, information technology can already provide some of the components of an electronic retail information system, for purposes of evaluation. In advertising, retailers and manufacturers can produce their catalogues in the form of *video cassettes* and *video discs* (see p. 67). Provided that would-be customers have at their disposal appropriate cassette or disc–replay equipment, these media add the possibility of motion and sound to existing forms of mail-order catalogues, at a comparable or lower cost.

Two-way telecommunication-based systems, such as videotex or *cable television*, can be used not only to advertise goods for sale but also to accept and acknowledge orders. The British Prestel system, for example, already has as information providers a number of retail organizations, and credit-card firms. Users of the system are able to order certain lines by authorizing the Prestel computer to supply their names and addresses to the retailer, together with other details of the order, which are keyed in by means of a numerical keyboard. In some cases, this facility is linked to the use of a credit card, with the keyboard again being used to enter the credit card number. A future development would allow the inclusion of detailed coloured photographs in the Prestel frame and so approximate the current form of pages of a mail-order catalogue.

With video cassettes, discs and videotex, the customer can look at the advertisements and respond to them (or not) at his or her leisure. With two-way cable television, the advertisement goes out 'live', just like any other tv commercial, and the customers are equipped with a keyboard, linked to the cable, with which they can indicate their interest in the item which is being broadcast.

Computer and telephone-based information systems, similar to Prestel, are also being used to give specialized services to the financial and commercial worlds. These systems carry up-to-the-minute information on stock prices, currency rates, world and national events, etc. Two of the largest of such systems are operated by international news agencies, Reuters and AP-Dow Jones. As with Prestel, information appears as text on tv-style display screens. Users are provided with full keyboards which enable them to originate information, as well as to select items of special interest to themselves. Both these systems are international, in the sense that the service is available in many countries.

Finance and commerce also have available to them all the information technology which is being developed for the 'electronic office'. Document preparation and distribution are just as much of concern to business as it is to administration. Electronic office aids such as telex, facsimile, text processing, computerized telephone exchanges, graphical input and output devices, voice input and output devices, conferencing via telephone, television (Fig. 2.7) or computer links have just as much potential in the business environment as in government offices. The impact of the 'microelectronic revolution' on finance and commerce has been most noticeable in making these products, as well as self-contained microcomputer systems, available to a wider range of businesses than before.

Fig. 2.7 Confravision, the audio-visual conference system pioneered by the British Post Office. It comprises a country-wide network of studios linked by closed-circuit television. There are also mobile studios. Display cameras are available in the studios to transmit pictures of graphs, maps, charts, documents and small objects. Among the uses of Confravision are business conferences, staff training, direct customer selling, market research and client presentation. Strict privacy can be maintained during an entire conference. (Post Office)

A new industry has also developed around the production of *computer programs* for the business users of most makes of microcomputer. Such *software packages* will increase in sophistication and reliability and form the basis of many information technology applications in this area (see p. 78).

The reliable and secure operation of computer and telecommunication-based systems is of particular importance in financial transactions. Errors in the processing and transmission of data can be expected to become less frequent as the technical quality of equipment improves, the reliability of software increases, and the equipment is designed with greater attention to the requirements and failings of people.

New information technology products will also have to contend with the problem of criminal misuse, such as wire-tapping or computer fraud. Methods and standards for dealing with this problem are currently under development in research laboratories. Some of these methods, and appropriate legislation, will also have a role in protecting the privacy of business transactions. They are discussed in the chapter on data protection (see p. 87).

Communication services

Under this rather broad heading is included the application of information technology in the telephone service, in broadcasting, and in specialist information services.

Telephone service

The telephone service is a vital component of many new systems and devices of information technology. Its quality, reliability, cost, and the range of facilities it offers are of major importance not only in its traditional role of providing a means of holding conversations at a distance, but also in the transmission of computer-compatible signals for whatever application.

At the present time the telephone systems of most countries are undergoing fundamental technical changes. At the heart of these changes lies the introduction of computers into telephone exchanges and into the telephones themselves.

The intention behind the computerization is to improve the performance of the national and international telephone networks (see p. 109). When the change-over is complete, towards the end of this century, the users are promised a faster, more reliable telephone service. There are also new facilities becoming available as a direct result of the computerization. These include:

(a) Abbreviated dialling—long telephone numbers, frequently called by a subscriber, can be obtained by dialling one or two digits.
(b) Repeat last call—a short code dialled after getting an engaged-tone automatically attempts again the last number dialled.
(c) Repeat last stored call—the number last dialled is put in a computer store (memory) so that other numbers can be dialled before attempting again the stored number.
(d) Divert calls—all incoming calls can be diverted automatically to a specified number; *or* this is done only after the original number does not answer after a given time; *or* only when the original number is engaged.
(e) Call waiting—incoming calls are acknowledged and asked to wait when the called number is engaged.
(f) Call barring—all incoming or all outgoing calls can be barred.
(g) Reminder calls—automatic call by the exchange at a requested time (as an alarm or reminder).
(h) Three-way connection—these can be set up from an ordinary phone.
(i) Remote control—all these facilities can be set up for the customer's own number from any other telephone.

The call-diversion facility is of particular interest since it will make possible a long-distance call for the price (to the caller) of a local call—the difference will be paid by the called party. The 'toll-free' or 800 calls in the USA already provide such a facility, to the advantage, for example, of commercial organizations which do not have to maintain a branch office in every city in order to answer inquiries or accept bookings.

During the period of introduction of these new facilities, there is likely to be a need for explanation and guidance about their use. The *computerized exchange* caters for this by offering an automatic 'talking guide' to help the user through a sequence of actions step-by-step.

The first British 'System X' computerized exchange was installed in July 1980 (see p. 60). In its first few months of operation it had a failure rate of one in 4000 calls, which is claimed to be 20 times better than some of the current range of electro-mechanical exchanges. The total cost of installing System X exchanges in place of the older types is £2.5 billion or nearly £700 000 for every *day* of the ten-year long project.

Another facility allows the two-way transmission of tv-like pictures along the telephone network. This would be of help, for example, in providing a visual element to *telephone conferences* (see p. 60)—link-ups between geographically distant locations. Another attractive development is the cordless telephone, linking to the network by means of a low-power radio transmitter. The telephone network itself is changing technically, beyond the use of computers in exchanges and telephones. The cables and wires which initially make up the transmission network are being supplemented by *optical-fibre* (light-guide) and *satellite transmission* links (see p. 55). For the user, the main effect of the introduction of these will be an increase in the number of circuits, or lines. Most of this increase is necessary to cater for a higher demand for telephone services (including data transmission, or computer-to-computer communication), but it is also intended to improve the quality and speed of service.

Broadcasting

The use of satellites for broadcast transmission is technically similar to their use as part of the international telephone network. The satellite effectively becomes a television transmitter in the sky. Instead of the 'herring-bone' aerial, a microwave dish is pointed at the satellite which appears to stand still 36 000 km (22 000 miles) overhead. The United States, the Soviet Union and several other countries already use satellites to relay tv programs. In Europe, Britain, France, West Germany, Italy, Switzerland and Luxembourg have plans to do so during the 1980s. Countries, other than those in North and South America, were each allocated five tv channels and a satellite slot in space by a special World Administrative Radio Conference, in 1977. A broadcast satellite for a nation can replace its entire ground-based television and radio transmitter network. Indeed, the coverage of a European satellite could transcend national boundaries, making it possible to gain access to hundreds of millions of people simultaneously. The microwave dish needed would be about 80 cm in diameter, and would cost about £100 to £200. A larger dish could supply a number of sets via a cable. A modern cable system can accommodate over 100 television channels, giving the viewer potential access to as many different sources of program material. Optical-fibre cables (to be considered in more detail in the chapter on optical communication systems, p. 63) promise a capacity of up to 1000 channels.

Once a cable is introduced into many homes, it can also be used to relay locally generated programs, as well as for the two-way transmission of electrical signals for music, surveillance, etc. In Britain, some of the delay in introducing satellite and cable services on a large scale is due to the recognized need to explore the social, environmental and financial implications of these developments.

Direct broadcasting apart, satellites have applications in military communications, navigation, scientific research and in business. In the military field, for example, satellite links assist in shipboard and submarine communication, while in the business field high-speed bulk data transfer, high-quality facsimile transmission, remote meetings, and other new services become possible. However, the costs of a broadcast satellite are substantial: a UK Home Office study in 1980 estimated the launch costs of a new service as £75m–£160m, depending on the type of satellite and the number of channels. Annual operating costs were estimated at £10m–£16m. On the other side of the coin, the manufacturers of equipment for direct satellite broadcasting estimate the world market to be several billions of pounds over the next 15 years.

Apart from the use of satellites and cables for relaying programs, the next few years will also see changes in the form and content of the information being broadcast. The trend is towards the use of digital (computer-compatible) signals, giving potentially better pictures and sound. The content of the transmitted signals will change by including additional components for services such as traffic information, program details, teletext-like services, etc.

Specialist information services

Information services devoted to specialist fields and professional interests are one of the fastest growing areas of information technology. Their expansion mirrors the growth in the amount of published items—books, periodicals, journals, reports, catalogues, manuals, audio and visual (film, television, photographic etc.) materials, patents, designs, computer programs—the records of human intellectual activity. Indeed, it has been estimated that the sum total of human knowledge is currently doubling every five years (Martin, J., *The Wired Society*, Prentice-Hall, 1978).

Such an exponential increase in potentially useful information would be impossible to handle without some new tools for its storage and retrieval. Conventional 'store-houses of knowledge', libraries, are running out of space and financial resources in trying to keep up with the output of recorded information. It is becoming virtually impossible for any particular library to possess every published item of information. Instead, libraries and entrepreneurial information services increasingly specialize on particular topics. Moreover, more and more of the information is being placed in *computerized data-bases* and/or recorded on microfilm.

Specialist computerized data-bases are now available in many countries. Access to them may be gained through computer terminals which either display the required information on their screen, or can be used to request a printed version. The terminals may be located anywhere that has a telecommunication link with the computer. For example, a data-base on educational publications is held in a computer system in California. It can be used, day or night, by account holders in any country via the international telephone network. Telecommunication costs tend to make the use of such computer-based information systems rather expensive for 'browsing', but again, technological changes are on the way. A recently introduced form of data transmission, called *packet switching*, can reduce the cost of using specialist data-bases at long distance (see p. 114). For example, a new service, Euronet-Diane, employs packet switching to link together a large number of hitherto separate data-bases in various western

European countries. An authorized user in any of the EEC countries will be able to link to any one of over 20 specialist data-bases, ranging from Italian judicial case law to the European Space Agency's reports. The information on tap covers a wide range of socio-economic, scientific and technical topics. In this way, the concept of a universal, world-wide store-house of knowledge is again becoming a possibility, this time through *data networks* (see p. 111) and the application of information science.

A recent development in videotex, the interlinking of Prestel with other computer data-bases through 'gateways', opens the door to these store-houses of information for a much wider public than hitherto (see p. 128).

Health care

Health care is an area where the applications of information technology have so far been on a rather small scale. The obvious uses of computers, in the administrative side of the operation of health services, have kept step with similar applications in other areas. Thus, personal records of hospital patients and of recipients of national health assistance are being maintained in data-banks in many western industrialized countries. However, the detailed medical, as opposed to general personal information held about people in such data-banks varies from country to country.

The confidentiality of medical records is the main consideration in such applications, and the wider use of computers for even this application is awaiting both improved security features in computerized data-bases and a clarification of laws and codes of practice on data protection. Even so, general practitioners can now use microcomputer-based filing systems and text-processing equipment for the day-to-day administration of their practice. The systems would deal with the financial accounts, lists and 'profiles' of patients, and would print reminders of appointments, repeat prescriptions, etc. These systems would be restricted to the practice itself, and the control of the data would remain with the general practitioner.

Another, well-publicized, application of computers in health care is computer tomography—the visualization of internal structures in the human body from data provided by an array of x-ray detectors (Fig. 2.8). The cost of the necessary equipment has so far proved to be a major stumbling block to the wide-spread use of this new technique. Computers are being used, on a limited scale, in applications such as the maintenance of abstracts of medical literature and medical statistics, the monitoring of critically ill patients who require continuous measurement of vital body functions, the automation of certain hospital laboratory tests, and diagnostic tests.

Computers are also being tested in the role of assistants in arriving at a diagnosis of the cause of patients' complaints. In some experiments, the patient answers questions posed by a computer terminal, in a conversational form; in others, the questions are posed by a doctor-figure on a video screen. In either case, the patient keys in the responses, which may be as simple as 'yes' or 'no'. The computer records these responses and comes up with a set of possible diagnoses, in order of their likelihood, for the doctor's consideration. In some systems, the computer holds a vast

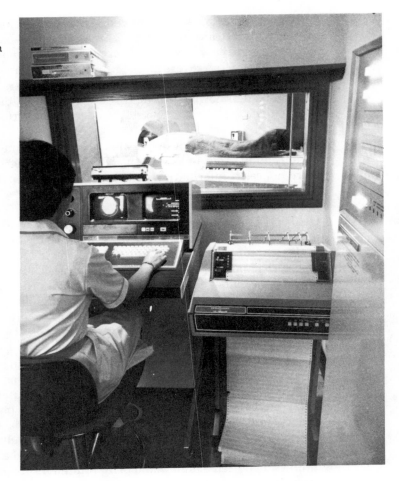

Fig. 2.8 Computer tomography. In this example, the patient's brain is being scanned by a ring of detectors. Their outputs are processed in a computer to give a picture of the cross-sectional structure of the brain. (International General Electric Company of New York Ltd)

amount of expert diagnostic experience, accumulated over a life-time by clinicians. Such an *expert system* (see p. 91) can be consulted by medical students, or doctors seeking a 'second opinion'. A variant on this theme is the computer system which allows medical students to experiment with treatment plans, examine the likelihood of various diagnoses, etc., using simulated medical cases.

Communication technology is also being employed in medical practice, on an experimental basis. It is possible, for example, to link medical electronic equipment used by patients in their homes, to a data recorder in a hospital via the telephone. In this way, routine tests on the patient, or on the equipment, can be performed at a distance. In a 'live' telecommunication link-up, using visual and audio channels, a doctor can examine a patient, admittedly only to a limited extent. But with the assistance of a trained nurse by the side of the patient, the range of tests can be extended. Such a system can be of significance where the doctors need to cover a large geographical area.

Information technology has also an important role to play in aiding people with sensory handicaps. There are already a large number of systems in use. Blind people, for example, would enormously benefit from having a device which converts printed text to speech. One such device, developed in the United States, scans the print with a beam of light at a rate of 150–200 words/min. A small computer associated with the device then applies about 1000 rules of grammar and pronunciation (with over 3000 exceptions to those rules). A *voice output* component then converts the resulting signals to comprehensible speech (see p. 101). This development suffers from a number of shortcomings, including its price (about $50 000), size, inability to cope with certain styles of print, newspapers, graphics, etc. However, none of these problems is technically insurmountable.

For those with impaired hearing, the arrival of *videotex* and *teletext* systems is of much significance (see p. 125). These systems can already provide a great deal of information in purely visual form, including subtitles for television programs. In the future, when videotex is developed to its full potential, deaf people will be able to use it to transmit messages person-to-person simply and rapidly. They would also benefit from low-cost *facsimile* (see p. 118), electronic publishing, *video discs* (see p. 70), and similar display-linked developments. There are many forecasts which put medical applications of information technology on the top of the list as the most rapidly expanding future markets. In view of the current level of usage, this may well be true. But in terms of cost-effectiveness and general acceptability, there is still a lot to be done.

Education and training

In comparison with the number of people involved in education and training, and with the size of the education budgets of most countries, the range of applications of information technology in these fields has so far been rather limited. However, the situation is gradually changing, partly as a result of the increasing accessibility of the products of information technology, and partly due to the need to educate and train people in the use of these new tools.

The most widely used educational technology medium is still *broadcasting*. A large proportion of schools is equipped with television and radio receivers, making use of special education programs transmitted by the public broadcasting stations. Many higher educational establishments are equipped with their own closed-circuit tv systems for the relay and recording of lectures, which can then be replayed as required. The Open Universities of Britain and of several other countries use broadcasting as a routine component of their distance-teaching system.

Video recording equipment (see p. 68) is often out of the reach of school budgets and, in any case, there is a shortage of good video-cassetted material not derived from broadcasts, which would justify the expenditure on such equipment. In complete contrast with schools, there is extensive use of video cassettes, and more recently of *video discs*, in industrial training, particularly in the United States. Business firms and other non-television organizations produced more such material there in 1977 for their own use than the program output of all commercial networks: some 46 000 programs totalling 15 000 h, at an estimated cost of more than $500 m. Twelve hundred major corporations are reported to be running their own private tv networks, and consider them cost-effective training media. The Ford Motor Company, for example, uses cassetted material for sales training, and General Motors has ordered over 10 000 video-disc players for in-house training (*Report of the US Joint Council on Educational Telecommunications*, January 1980).

The United States is also leading the way in the application of two-way telecommunication media in education: two-way cable-tv and the telephone. *Two-way cable* provides a return channel to a tutor in a remote location who can monitor the students' progress with the video material and offer assistance, vision or voice, as necessary. This is, however, an expensive medium for routine educational purposes and no wide-spread use is expected until a technological advance (such as the wide-spread installation of optical-fibre cables and the use of broadcast satellites) changes the economic equation. With *satellite links* becoming available in some parts of the world, particularly in North America, they are being incorporated into educational provision. Their main use is in areas which, for geographical reasons, are difficult to supply with ordinary broadcast services. Currently, operational systems include Alaska, the Rocky Mountains, and the Appalachian region of the USA. In addition, satellite transmission is being used experimentally for *video conferencing*, i.e. for two or multi-way audio and tv link-ups. This enables a teacher in one location to see, talk and listen to students in one or more remote locations. One such system operates between Stanford in California and Quebec in Canada.

A less costly form of two or multi-way live long-distance link between teacher and student is provided by the *telephone network*. Teaching by telephone is being used on a routine basis in the American state of Wisconsin. The University of Wisconsin provides an Extension Service (i.e. off-campus degree courses) in 20 locations around the state via a dedicated telephone network. The courses are aimed at the adult population, and include professional up-dating and other continuing education courses. The cost of operating the service works out at about $20 per student contact hour. Half of this cost is borne by the student. A recent survey shows that around 40 different institutions are using telephone teaching in the USA.

In Britain, the Open University has long been operating telephone tutorials, both for groups of students at the University's study centres, and for individual students participating from their home, but linked up in a multi-way *telephone conference* (see p. 60). Again, this method of bringing together tutor and student is most appropriate in distance education where geographical separation virtually precludes any other form of direct contact. One important shortcoming of telephone conferencing in educational applications is the lack of visual aids. To overcome this problem, yet to keep costs low, the Open University has recently developed a 'remote blackboard' device (Fig. 2.9). This uses the telephone line to transmit pictures drawn by the tutor or the student on the screen of an ordinary tv set by means of a light-pen. So, a tutor can deliver a conventional lecture or tutorial from his or her home to the home of students who can, in turn, ask questions or draw their own diagrams in a fully interactive mode. The Open University device, like many other recent products of technology, has only become a

Fig. 2.9 The Cyclops system developed at the Open University, Milton Keynes. Handwritten or printed text and graphics can be transmitted from one Cyclops terminal to another via the public telephone network, or can be recorded (and replayed) in sound-coded form on an ordinary cassette recorder. The Cyclops' tv screen can be used as a blackboard. The user 'writes' on it with a light pen, and is able to edit the picture if necessary. In this way, a tutor and one or more groups of students can 'write' and 'draw' to another. (Open University)

cost-effective proposition because of the availability of low-cost microelectronic circuits. The same trend has also led to the availability of computing equipment for educational purposes at prices which put it in the range of school budgets.

In Britain, government aid has been made available to schools, in terms of matching funds, for the purchase of *microcomputer* systems. The aim is for every secondary school to have at least one computer available to use by 1983. Other western industrialized countries are also moving towards 'computer literacy' in schools. In the USA, for example, there were about 50 000 computers installed in schools in 1980, and this number is expected to rise to 200 000 by 1985.

It is clear, however, that the provision of computing equipment alone is not sufficient to achieve this goal. Two other conditions must be fulfilled: the integration of the computer into the curriculum, and the availability of programs of high educational standard which exploit the processing and data-storage power of the computer to the full. Both these conditions depend, in turn, on the willingness and ability of teachers to use the computer as an everyday teaching tool. A significant investment is being made by computer hardware manufacturers to make the computer more attractive to teachers, and government money is also being made available for the training of teachers in computer skills.

A well-known example of manufacturer support for an educational use of both computer and telecommunication technologies is the Plato system. This was developed at the University of Illinois in the 1970s, with the support of the Control Data Corporation, a major American computer manufacturer. Plato uses its own very powerful large computers, its own telecommunication network, and even its own specially developed student terminals. In the early years of the development, when the project also received US government support, a great deal of computer-based instruction material was developed for Plato. Computer-based instruction (as opposed to computer-assisted learning) has been found to be more applicable to industrial and other training situations than to school education, and it is in training that Plato has had most of its success.

While Plato represents an approach to computer training based on the idea of a vast and powerful centralized computer serving a large number of terminals via a communication network, the more recent school microcomputers are 'stand-alone' devices. That is, just like the text processors of the business world, they contain sufficient processing power and memory to operate independently of other computers. However, just like text processors, some of the educational microcomputers can be interconnected through *local networks* (see p. 111). In this way, they may share more expensive and larger capacity data-storage devices and printers, and also enable the teacher to monitor and help with the work of individual students through a central console. This parallel of the educational and business applications of information technology illustrates a more general trend in the penetration of new technology: education is not the first area to adopt such developments. It is only when a technology becomes robust, cheap and extensively available that the educational world is prepared to consider its use on a routine basis.

The home

Applications of information technology in the home have so far centred on three main areas: telecommunication, entertainment, and news services.

Two-way telecommunication is based almost entirely on the telephone network, although in some countries *cable television* and citizen-band radio have been used for this purpose. Although initially intended only for voice communication, the telephone network is now increasingly used to convey also other forms of information. By linking computer terminals or videotex equipment to the telephone socket, distant computer data-bases can be accessed from the home. In this way, people whose work involves using a computer or who wish to look up general or special interest information contained in data-stores can do so without leaving their home.

The provision of entertainment and news have, up to recently, tended to be the exclusive province of the broadcasting and printed publishing media. Now, the *video cassette* and *video disc* (see p. 70) provide alternative sources of entertainment material, and *teletext* and *videotex* services (see p. 125) bring instantaneous, up-to-the-minute news into the home. These services are also taking over some of the public awareness, advertising, and features functions of newspapers and magazines, so far in a small way.

The transition from these products and services of today to some possible future applications of information technology in the home is marked by the promise of low-cost microelectronic systems. Already on the horizon are home computers for uses other than the conventional computing tasks. Their use as entertainment devices is already with us, in the form of computer games of increasing sophistication and even of

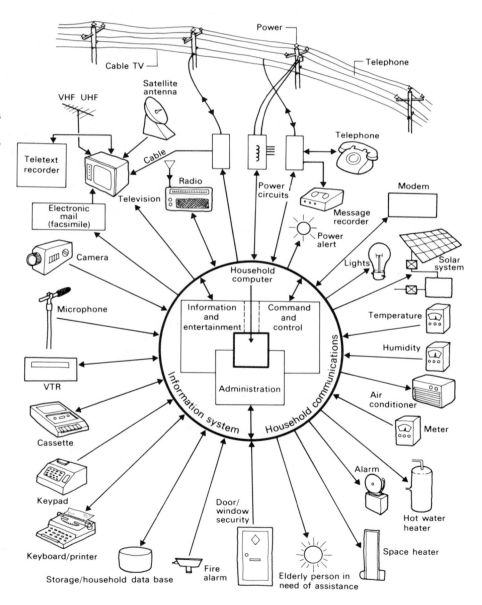

Fig. 2.10 A computer-centred view of the home information ring-main. The computer acts as the central control panel and communication centre for other electronic equipment in the home. (Adapted from Carne, 1980, 'The wired household', *IEEE Spectrum*, October, p. 65, © 1980 IEEE)

some educational content. They will also serve as a means of *aids to learning* of a more serious type, giving a semblance of a one-to-one relationship between tutor and learner. When linked to other computers via a two-way telecommunication medium, the home computer will gain access to a range of services already discussed in this section. These include text processing at-a-distance, *electronic mail* (see p. 117), electronic funds transfer, medical assistance, and distance-learning facilities. They will also be able to make use of computer programs (software packages) from centralized 'program warehouses' or from specialist suppliers. *Voice input* and *output* (see p. 101), links to home security devices (detectors, locks, etc.) and to other domestic equipment (lights, heating and ventilation control, etc.) for personal computers are also becoming a reality, at least technically, if not economically.

One view of how a 'home information and control centre' of the future may operate comes from the United States (Carne, 'The wired household', *IEEE Spectrum*, October 1980, p. 65). It is summarized in Fig. 2.10. The computer occupies the central position in this picture. It communicates with other equipment by means of a *local network* of electric or optical-fibre cable, and with the outside world by broadcast signals, and digital signals via a *data network* (see p. 107). One application envisaged for such a centre is 'electronic shopping'. Already, it is possible to use the telephone for mail-ordering and payment authorization. In the United States, one mail-order company's computer can be linked, via the telephone network, to home computers, and a two-way cable-tv service is available.

The usefulness of interlinking domestic appliances in this way is yet to be proved. There are also several technical, economic and social hurdles in the way of the home information centre: for example, many households are still without telephone, let alone equipped with the wide-band cable needed for fast, high-volume electronic communication. The economic justification for many of the new products and services will only exist if they are able to offer savings compared with existing ways, or if they satisfy a hitherto unfulfilled need. The social problems that may be raised by such development include reduced face-to-face contact, and the need to protect personal communication from accidental or criminal misuse.

Summary

A common feature of the current range of tools offered by information technology is that they represent an *alternative* to established media and to existing facilities for handling information. By converting the *form* in which information is expressed to the digital form used by computers, they make it possible to combine a range of tasks hitherto done as separate operations. For example, text translated to this form does not have to be typed out or duplicated when it passes from one person, or section, in an organization to another. Rather, it is the electronic signals representing that text which are transmitted, filed, modified or displayed, using the new tools and products developed for those purposes.

Whether the alternative offered by information technology is a solution to recognized problems or whether it is an answer in search of questions is the subject of much current discussion. In some areas, such as banking, communications and certain military applications, the amount of information that needs to be handled, or the time available for its processing, make it necessary to employ the electronic alternative. In other areas, such as the home, medicine, education, information technology is yet to make a serious impact. In a third group of applications, in the office, in manufacturing industries, in commerce, the new technology is on trial. Its capacity for performing some of the more mechanical, menial tasks currently done by people is at once its strength and threat.

The use of electronic signals does not provide, in itself, a more attractive alternative to long-established tools of human information handling. If anything, it interposes an additional link in the communication chain, with its attendant 'interface' problems. The contribution of electronic (and optical) representations of information lies in the speed, reliability and reduced physical storage requirements associated with these representations. Furthermore, the existence of automatic equipment (e.g. computers) for the processing of electronic signals holds out the prospect of the automation of tasks which involve representations of information.

There is still a great deal to be learned about information, its use by people and the way people interact with machines before information technology can realize its *full* potential as an aid to human communication and decision-making.

Part 2

3 Introduction

Part 1 has pointed to a range of products and systems which form the 'technology' component of information technology. Table 3.1 summarizes these, in the context of the applications where they are mentioned. The crosses in the table refer to a specific mention of a product or system in Chapter 2. The absence of a cross does not mean that a particular pairing is of no interest to information technology. Indeed, a striking feature of the table is the way in which a key new development is adapted, perhaps with slight variations, to a wide variety of uses. So, even if Chapter 2 has not given examples of all possible combinations of products and applications, such combinations may have already been tried or could be tried in the future.

The row entries of Table 3.1 represent the author's choice of areas of information technology for further discussion. The choice is to some extent arbitrary but the areas between them cover both the historical basis and the most recent growth areas of information technology. The ordering of topics in the table is alphabetic to exclude implications of their relative importance. However, such a neutral listing also disguises the logical relationship between the various areas. In a historical and didactic sense, the key areas are telecommunications and computers. Their subsequent convergence has given rise to data networks, as shown in Fig. 3.1. The other row entries of Table 3.1 represent some of the

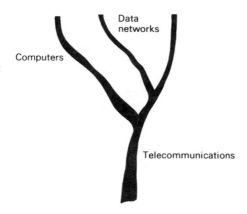

Fig. 3.1 The 'information technology tree'. The 'trunk' of the tree is telecommunications whose history goes back to the last quarter of the 19th century. The computer 'branch' dates from the mid-20th century, and data communications about 10 years later

off-shoots of the main branches of the 'information technology tree'. Figure 3.2 is an attempt to show their relationship to the three main branches. The chapters which follow reflect this structure by their ordering.

Fig. 3.2 New branches of the 'information technology tree'

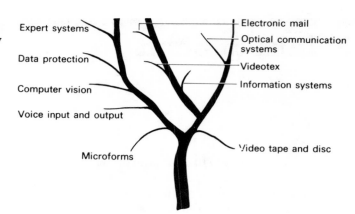

Expert systems

Data protection

Computer vision

Voice input and output

Microforms

Electronic mail

Optical communication systems

Videotex

Information systems

Video tape and disc

Table 3.1 Some products and systems of information technology, and their applications identified in Part 1.

	Office	Industry	Commerce and finance	Communication services	Health care	Education	Home
Computers	✕	✕	✕	✕	✕	✕	✕
Input devices	✕		✕		✕		
Output devices	✕	✕	✕		✕		
Storage	✕						
Software		✕	✕			✕	✕
Computer vision	✕	✕	✕				
Data networks	✕	✕	✕	✕			✕
Local networks	✕	✕					✕
Long-distance networks			✕	✕	✕	✕	
Data protection	✕	✕	✕	✕	✕	✕	✕
Electronic mail	✕	✕	✕	✕			✕
Expert systems					✕	✕	
Information systems	✕	✕	✕	✕		✕	
Microforms	✕	✕					
Optical communication systems				✕			✕
Telecommunications	✕	✕	✕	✕	✕	✕	✕
Cable tv			✕	✕		✕	✕
Computer-controlled exchanges	✕	✕	✕	✕			
Satellite systems	✕	✕		✕		✕	✕
Telephone networks	✕	✕	✕	✕	✕	✕	✕
Video tape disc systems	✕	✕	✕		✕	✕	✕
Videotex and teletext	✕	✕	✕	✕			✕
Voice communication with computers	✕	✕	✕	✕	✕	✕	✕

4 Telecommunications

Introduction and fundamentals

The main purpose of telecommunications is to transmit representations of information (*signals*) between remote locations. Most telecommunication systems in operation today employ electrical or electromagnetic media (including light waves) as carriers of signals. These media are harnessed to provide world-wide telecommunication networks. The characteristics of the signals to be transmitted (which will be our first concern below) largely determine the type of network (e.g. data networks, television networks, etc.), while practical engineering and economic considerations dictate the choice of transmission medium (e.g. metal or optical-fibre cables, etc.) and whether a transmission link is dedicated to a particular use, or as is more often the case, it is shared among a number of users, e.g. in switched networks used for speech or videotex.

The main components of a telecommunication system are shown diagrammatically in Fig. 4.1. They include *terminals* which convert

Fig. 4.1 **A** telecommunication network used for speech transmission requires equipment to convert between speech and its electrical signal representation. The electrical signals are used in the transmission and routing processes

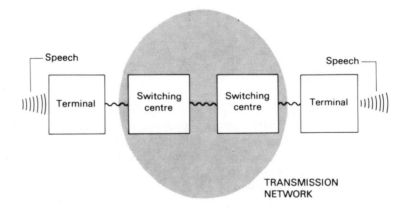

representations of information to, and from, the form used within the system and other forms used outside it. The telephone is an example of a terminal, converting the acoustic waves of speech into a fluctuating electrical signal, and the signal back to audible form. The network contains *transmission paths* and *switching centres*, so that the terminals can exchange messages with each other, and optionally, with terminals of other telecommunication systems, through inter-network links.

This generalized view of the network assumes that the terminals connected to the network are capable of acting both as senders and as receivers of signals (a telephone, for example, is equipped with both a microphone and a loudspeaker enabling it to act in *one-to-one*,

one-to-many or *many-to-many* link-ups). Some systems, such as public broadcast networks, provide only a central sender and many receivers in a *one-to-all* configuration. In such a configuration, there is no need for switching centres.

Signals and terminals

Representations of information (speech, text, pictures, measurements, etc.) must be converted to signals for the purpose of telecommunication. Signals themselves are also representations appropriate to the medium which has been chosen as the carrier. A signal is usually represented by the *variation* of some property of the carrier with respect to time. For example, the variations in electrical current representing speech in a telephone system may look as shown in Fig. 4.2. These variations mimic

Fig. 4.2 An analogue signal can take on values from a continuous range of possible values over a length of time

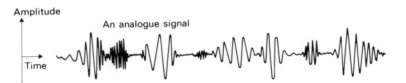

the changes in air pressure at the microphone. Both the air pressure and the electrical signal can vary over a continuous range of possible values; they are called *analogue* representations.

An example of the other main type of signal is that used within computers, as a means of internal communication. It is of the form of electrical pulses (Fig. 4.3) which can take only a finite number of values

Fig. 4.3 A digital signal can take on only a limited set of possible values (one of only two values for a binary signal) and transitions between these values occur rapidly

(in this case two) from a discontinuous range. These are *digital* signals.

The distinction between analogue and digital signals has been expressed in terms of the size of the variation of the carrier (also called the *amplitude* of the signal). But there is also the other dimension of variation—time. The rapidity (rate) of variation of either type of signal determines the *bandwidth* occupied by it (see also p. 108). Bandwidth is expressed on a scale of frequencies, and is measured in units of hertz (Hz), thousands of hertz (kHz), millions of hertz (MHz), etc. Human speech has a bandwidth of about 4 kHz, orchestral music about 15 kHz, a colour tv (video) signal, on the 625-line system, about 5.5 MHz, and on 525-line systems, about 4.2 MHz.

The bandwidth of a digital signal depends on the duration of the shortest pulse used in the particular application. This determines the maximum number of pulses that can be sent per unit time. If the unit of time is the second then the pulse rate is expressed in *bauds*. In most computer applications, where the representation is based on a pulse being present or absent, the pulse rate in bauds is the same as the number of data *bits* per second. (A bit is an elementary data unit, a 1 or a 0.) Teletypewriter terminals normally operate at data rates of 110 or

300 bit/s, but at the other extreme, parts of the computer can communicate with each other at data rates of several Mbit/s (1 Mbit/s = 1 million bit/s).

Terminals act as the interface between the source/destination of a message and the network. They must be able to reproduce, or convert, the form of representation of a message without appreciable distortion. Table 4.1 gives examples of terminals which match particular types of message source/destination to particular transmission media and signal representations.

Table 4.1 Examples of telecommunication (Source: Smol et al., *Telecommunications—A Systems Approach*, Allen and Unwin, 1976)

Type of communication	Message source	Transmitter terminal	Transmission channel	Receiver terminal	Destination
Own-exchange telephone call	Speech	Telephone	Local lines and exchange	Telephone	Human listener
Transatlantic telephone call	Speech	Telephone	Local and trunk lines, local, trunk and international exchanges, communication satellite or submarine cable	Telephone	Human listener
Public broadcast radio	Speech and music	Studio, rf transmitter and links between the two	Radio waves	Radio receiver	Human listener
Telegraph	Human operator	Teletypewriter	Lines (wire pairs) and exchanges	Teletypewriter	Human addressee
Data link to a computer	Human operator or paper tape	Teletypewriter and modem	200 baud data link	Modem and computer input/output devices	Computer

Transmission media

The media used to carry representations of messages differ widely in physical form, speed, capacity and the fidelity with which they are capable of transmitting messages. Engineers are in constant search of physical phenomena, and methods of their utilization, which can lead to faster, cheaper, more faithful transmission of signals.

The fastest transmission media operate at the speed of light, 300 million m/s. The two most widely used forms can be classified as *bounded media* and *free space*. Both make use of electromagnetic wave propagation as the carrier of signals. Bounded media include twisted pairs of wires, coaxial cables, waveguides, optical fibres (light-guides), illustrated in Fig. 4.4. Free space is utilized for transmission between aerials (antennas), or radiation sources and sensors. The fidelity of transmission in these media is dependent on the signal being able to retain its pertinent characteristics (shape, bandwidth, etc.). The main factors influencing this are the effective *bandwidth of the medium* and *noise*.

The concept of the bandwidth of a medium is similar to that of a signal: it is the range of frequencies which it can transmit efficiently (the 'efficiency' being strictly defined in engineering terms). That is, for a signal of a given bandwidth to be transmitted with a defined fidelity by a

Fig. 4.4 Some examples of bounded transmission media:

(a) Twisted pairs of wires formed into a cable
(b) Coaxial cables: submarine type (top) and underground type (bottom)
(c) Waveguides: metal tubes, about 7.5 cm in diameter

(From 'Communication channels', Henri Busignies. Copyright © 1972 by Scientific American, Inc. All rights reserved)

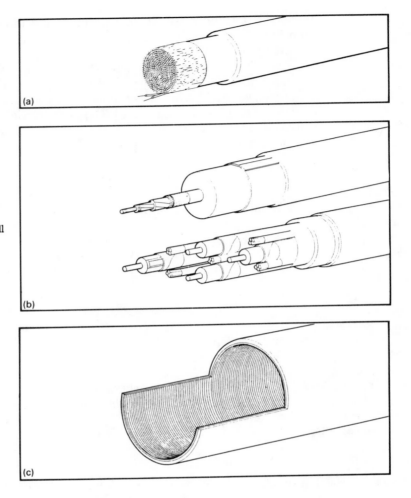

medium, the bandwidth of the signal must be within the bandwidth of the medium. As an example, Fig. 4.5 shows the range of frequencies present in human speech. By experience, it has been found that speech remains comprehensible even if its bandwidth is electronically limited to 3.5 kHz. So, in telephone transmission, the bandwidth of each speech circuit is engineered to be 4 kHz. In this way, it can contain the (truncated) bandwidth of speech together with a small 'guard-band' to cater for imperfections in truncation and transmission.

The notion of the bandwidth of a medium is complicated by the fact that its value is dependent upon distance from the source. The bandwidth gets smaller with increasing distance, unless devices known as repeaters are used to compensate for this effect. For example, with repeaters, twisted pairs of wires can have a bandwidth of 500 kHz over some 75 km. Without repeaters, the effective bandwidth drops from about 100 kHz at 1 km to virtually zero at 75 km. Coaxial cables, with a repeater spacing of 1.5 km, can have an effective bandwidth of over 60 MHz, while waveguides with an effective bandwidth of more than 2000 MHz have

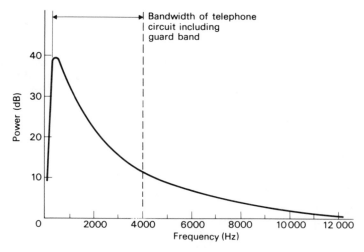

Fig. 4.5 Human speech is represented here by the intensity (power) of vibrations at different frequencies. Superimposed is the bandwidth of speech circuits in telephone transmission

been fabricated. Optical fibres are still in the research and development phase but fibres of 100 MHz effective bandwidth at 1 km have been demonstrated.

Communication satellites, which use free space as the transmission medium, can provide up to 2300 MHz bandwidth in the current range of Intelsat 5 satellites, compared with the bandwidth of 50 MHz of Intelsat 1 launched in 1965. Unfortunately, the length of a satellite link (about 35 000 km each way) is such that the returning signal is very weak, hardly distinguishable from noise. To exploit the full bandwidth, expensive ground-station equipment is required.

Noise, the other important factor affecting transmission, takes on a special meaning in the field of telecommunications. It includes all the unwanted signals which corrupt the message signal. Noise may be due to electronic components, say in the transmitter or repeater, or to natural disturbances.

The relative strengths of the message signal and of noise in a transmission link determine the maximum rate at which it can transmit signals without error. This maximum rate, which is also dependent on the bandwidth of the link, is called the *capacity* of the link. The mathematical expression which defines capacity in terms of these quantities is known as Shannon's law (Shannon, 'Mathematical theory of communication', *Bell System Technical Journal*, July/October 1948, p. 401). The theoretical capacity of a transmission link is seldom even approached in practice. An important reason for this is the cost and complexity of the necessary terminal equipment, which has to separate the wanted signal from the unwanted noise. When added to the cost of the link itself (e.g. the coaxial cable or satellite construction and launch costs), the investment needed to establish a long-distance telecommunication network is quite substantial. (It represents about two-thirds of the total cost of the system.)

One way of exploiting the bandwidth of transmission links more effectively is by accommodating more than one signal in the available

Multiplexing

Multiplexing is the use of a single telecommunication link to transmit a number of different signals, either simultaneously or in rapid succession.

As shown in Fig. 4.6, a telecommunication link may be visualized as a medium with some bandwidth, available over a length of time. If each of the signals to be transmitted requires a smaller capacity than that available in the link, the available capacity may be split up either into (a) frequency bands or (b) time bands, as shown in Fig. 4.7.

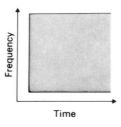

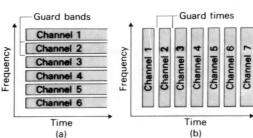
(a)   (b)

In frequency-division multiplexing, electronic frequency translators (modulators and demodulators) are used to ensure that individual signals occupy their allocated channels. The widths of the channels need not be the same—optimum utilization of the link results if each channel occupies only the bandwidth it requires.

Fig. 4.6 A tele-communication channel can be represented by its bandwidth available over a length of time

Fig. 4.7 The tele-communication channel of Fig. 4.6 can be fully utilized in one of two ways:

(a) By subdividing it into narrower frequency bands, or channels
(b) By allocating its full bandwidth to a set of channels in turn

bandwidth. This is done by a technique known as *multiplexing* (see panel above, also p. 109). Multiplexing is the sharing of a wide-band link among signals of narrower bandwidth requirements. For example, as noted earlier, a single-speech signal in the telephone network requires a bandwidth of 3.5 kHz. The various transmission media used in telephone networks have bandwidths much in excess of this, so they are split into *channels* of 4 kHz bandwidth (again with a 'safety margin') for better utilization. A waveguide with a 2000 MHz bandwidth, say, could be split up in this way into about half a million speech channels, each carrying a different speech signal. To slot into these channels, the speech signals are modified electronically (by *modulation*) at, or after leaving, the transmitter and unscrambled (by *demodulation*) at, or before reaching, the receiver (see panel opposite). The process of tuning a radio or tv receiver to a particular station is just the selection of a particular channel out of the many which share out the available bandwidth. (The vhf band,

Modulation

Modulation is the variation of some characteristic of a signal (called the carrier signal) in accordance with the instantaneous value of another signal (the modulating signal).

If the carrier signal is a sine wave, as shown in Fig. 4.8, the

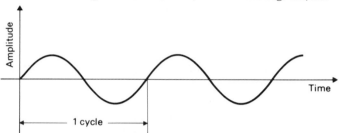

Fig. 4.8 A sine wave is characterized in terms of its amplitude (instantaneous value), frequency (number of repetitions of the wave per second) and phase (starting point relative to some timing mark)

characteristics which may be varied include its amplitude, frequency and phase, corresponding to amplitude modulation (am), frequency modulation (fm) and phase modulation (pm), respectively. These are illustrated in Fig. 4.9 for the case of a modulating signal which is a sequence of pulses.

Fig. 4.9 Three methods of modulating a carrier sine wave by a digital modulating signal:

(a) Amplitude modulation. A binary 1 corresponds to a higher amplitude than binary 0

(b) Frequency modulation. A binary 1 corresponds to a lower frequency of oscillation than binary 0.

(c) Phase modulation. A binary 1 corresponds to a sine wave whose phase is one half cycle different from that of a sine wave representing binary 0.

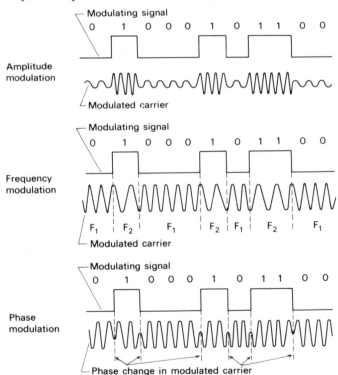

The carrier signal itself may be a train of pulses. In that case, called pulse-code modulation (pcm), the characteristics available for variation include the amplitude, width, phase, position and number of pulses.

The purpose of modulation is to translate or code the modulating signal so that it becomes better matched to the available transmission link. At the receiving end of the link, the signal is recovered, or demodulated, electronically.

for example, is 270 MHz wide, and is divided into channels each 200 kHz wide.)

The improved utilization of a transmission link by means of multiplexing is not the only way of sharing out its capacity. An additional possibility is to allocate each channel to a new user when the current user no longer requires it. This is achieved by connecting different terminals to the channels, in other words by *switching*.

Switched networks

The need for switching arises in a network when more than about a handful of terminals are connected to it. The reason for this is illustrated in Fig. 4.10 for the case of ten terminals. Figure 4.10(a) shows that, to enable each terminal to communicate with all others, it is necessary to provide 45 links. The number of links increases disproportionately with the number of terminals; for example, for 100 terminals, 4950 links are needed, while for the total number of telephones in use in Britain today the number of links would run to 15 digits.

Figure 4.10(b) illustrates that if each of the original ten lines is connected to a switching centre, instead of directly to each other, the number of lines reduces to ten. Note that this approach will not reduce the number of possible interconnections, it merely cuts the number of transmission channels.

Figure 4.10(c) shows a further improvement: the individual lines between the terminals and the switching centre can be reduced in length by introducing more switching centres, local to a group of terminals, and linking these by trunk lines. The trunks are just wide-band links which can carry a large number of channels along the same link. In large networks, such as a national telephone network, the trunks themselves may be switched, for example, to offer alternative routings and so to improve the reliability of the network. This usually results in a hierarchical arrangement of lines and switching centres (exchanges), as shown in Fig. 4.11. The analogy here is to the road or railway network of a country: the switching centres can be likened to major road or railway junctions, and the trunk lines to the inter-city road or railway routes.

A switching centre may be visualized as a large number of electrical contacts, each of which may be open or closed, forming a switching network (see Fig. 4.12). The action of each switch is under the control of a control unit. The switches are so organized that any line connected to the centre, including trunk lines, can be connected to any other line, in a temporary manner. This latter restriction is because, for practical and economic reasons, the number of switches is less than that required to interlink all the lines, in pairs, at the same time. So, the same switches are shared out among successive calls. The size of the switching network determines the number of simultaneous calls an exchange can handle.

Switching centres have gone through a century of development, from the early manual exchanges to the modern automatic, computerized exchanges. Computers are employed in some of the present-day exchanges in the role of the control unit. This is known as *stored-program control* (spc). In an even smaller number of ultra-modern exchanges (but an increasing number of future ones) the switching network is also

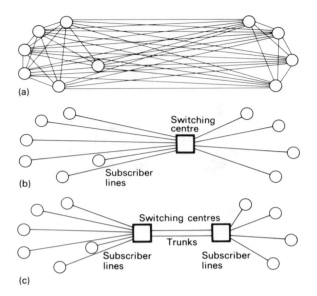

Fig. 4.10 Three possible arrangements for a small network:

(a) Direct connection between the terminals, requiring many lines
(b) The use of a switching centre reduces the required number of lines to the number of terminals
(c) Local switching centres may be interconnected by trunk lines

Fig. 4.11 The national telephone network is organized in tiers. The international network is structured similarly.

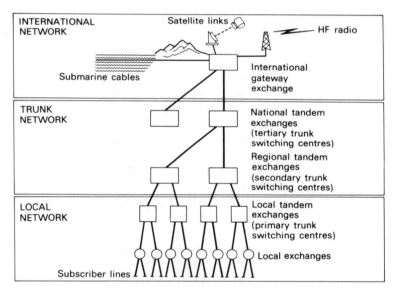

computerized. The technical name for this is *digital switching*. It is particularly applicable where all signals travelling in the network, including the speech signals, are digital in form. The long-term plans of many telecommunication organizations include the conversion of the present analogue-signal transmission network to an all-digital-signal data network. The conversion, however, has to be a gradual one, owing to the scale of the task, and its cost. This means that the switching centres being introduced now will have to cater for both analogue and digital signals, as the amortization time of a large switching centre is 20 to 30 years. An example of this dual-purpose switching centre is the British System X range of exchanges.

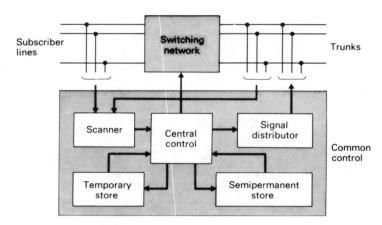

Fig. 4.12 An electronic telephone exchange. The switching network (at top) is controlled by the common control unit (shaded box). The scanner monitors the incoming subscribers' and trunk lines. The data relating to calls in progress are stored in the temporary store. General procedures for establishing calls are stored as computer programs in the semi-permanent store. Pairs of lines are connected and disconnected in the switching network. The signal distributor supplies the dialing, engaged, ringing and other tones. (From 'Communication networks', Hiroshi Inose. Copyright © 1972 by Scientific American, Inc. All rights reserved)

System X

System X is a collection of equipment and computer program modules which can be combined together in various configurations to produce switching centres in a range of sizes, for different applications. The range of sizes extends from 24 lines to 85 000, and the applications from a simple multiplexer to a large trunk exchange or international network switching centre. The larger exchanges can handle up to 500 000 busy-hour call attempts.

The exchanges use distributed microprocessors, stored-program control, and digital switching (within the system, speech is handled as digital signals, with any necessary conversion and reconversion performed by special modules). The exchange modules are capable of being interfaced to analogue-signal lines, and to digital-signal lines operating up to 2.048 Mbit/s, equivalent to 30 speech channels at 64 kbit/s each, including optical-fibre links.

Applications

Telecommunication services are at the heart of many applications of information technology. In the office setting, the internal telephone network is based on wire-pairs or cables, linked to a private (in-house) exchange, with a wide range of facilities, not always found in public networks. These may include automatic call transfers, signalling urgent calls arriving when another call is in progress (this may then be taken while the original call is on 'hold'), call monitoring, automatic dialling, abbreviated dialling of long or frequently used numbers, paging, pre-recorded messages, automatic answering, dictation recording, etc.

One service of particular interest to many organizations with offices or branches on distant sites or those wishing to replace travel by telecommunications is *telephone conferencing*. This facility is available on many private exchanges and, via the operator, on the public network as well. It involves the interlinking of more than two parties in a single call, so that everyone can hear everyone else. At any site there may be a single participant, using an ordinary telephone, or a group of people with a loud-speaking telephone. Pushbutton-activated light signals can be used to indicate to the chairman that a participant wishes to speak. Other signals may control local visual or graphic display media which show previously distributed illustrations.

One method of distributing documents or graphical information in advance of telephone conferences is facsimile transmission (discussed in greater detail on p. 118). Another is *slow-scan television* transmitted over the telephone network. Alternatively, a telephone conference may be combined with a video (television) conference link so that the participants can see each other and view presentations involving movement. Unfortunately, the cost of multi-site conferences of this type is still quite high, and the technical and human problems have not been fully resolved. With the wider-scale introduction of digital wide-band networks and computerized exchanges into the public telecommunication network, the cost and technical problems at least may find a solution.

In industrial environments, remote control and measurement form an increasingly important application area for telecommunications. They make it possible to monitor and control equipment in hostile or dangerous situations, at unmanned and remote locations, etc. In financial and commercial applications, telecommunication is already widely employed for ordering, business negotiations, news and wire services, message transmission, etc. The services discussed in the chapter on electronic mail (p. 119) are also relevant here, and in the previous two application areas. Electronic funds transfer and direct-mail ordering systems are likely to become major future users of telecommunication services. In the field of communications, the public telephone and broadcast systems will expand, but are also likely to be joined by privately operated ('value-added') services, exploiting the wide-band transmission facilities of cable networks and telecommunication satellites. The development of microcomputer-based telephones and exchanges will provide an increasing range of facilities to telephone users.

The educational and health services are so far not major users of telecommunications. However, with other technological developments, applications such as education and training at a distance, better assistance to the disabled and elderly, access to remote information sources, become possible. For the home user, improved telecommunications may mean a reduction in information-related travel.

Further reading

Flood, J. E. (ed.). (1975). *Telecommunication Networks*, Peter Peregrinus.
de Sola Pool, I. (ed.). (1977). *The Social Impact of the Telephone*, MIT Press.
Johansen, R., Vallee, J. and Spangler, K. (1979). *Electronic Meetings: Technical Alternatives and Social Choices*, Addison-Wesley.
Martin, J. (1977). *Future Developments in Telecommunications*, 2nd edn., Prentice-Hall.
Martin, J. (1978). *Satellite Communication Systems*, Prentice-Hall.
Smol, G., Hamer, M. and Hills, M. (1976). *Telecommunications—A Systems Approach*, George Allen & Unwin.

5 Optical communication systems

Introduction and fundamentals

Optical communication systems are a recent addition to the armoury of telecommunication systems. (The first commercially viable systems appeared only in the 1970s.) Their main use so far has been in data networks (see p. 107).

They exploit light as the carrier of information (in contrast to electrical signals in electronic communication systems) and optical fibres as the medium for transmitting the light signals (analogous to wires and cables in electrical transmission). Additionally, light waves can be used for the direct transmission of signals, just as radio waves are employed to transmit conventional broadcasts. However, the direct form of optical communication has limited use because of its short range (a few kilometres).

Most optical communication systems in current use are linked to established electronic communication networks and devices. The conversion of signals from one form to the other is carried out by special coupling components. Figure 5.1 shows the main parts of an optical-fibre

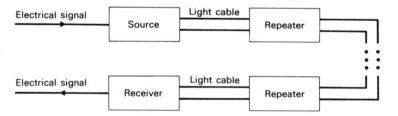

Fig. 5.1 An optical fibre telecommunication link requires equipment to convert between electrical signals and light, and repeaters to boost (electronically) the pulses travelling along the optical-fibre cable

communication system interfaced to an electronic system. Electronic signals are converted to pulses of light, in the infrared range, by a *source* (e.g. a light-emitting diode or a laser). The light is picked up by one or more optical fibres which may be linked end-to-end. At the far end, light is reconverted to electronic signals by a *receiver* (a photodetector). Signals can be transmitted in either direction, provided, of course, that both ends of the fibre are equipped with a source and a receiver. If transmission is to take place over distances in excess of some 10 km, the light signals need regenerating in *repeaters*. This is because light is absorbed to some extent in the optical fibre. The fibre conducts light by virtue of its transparency (it is made of glass or, in some applications, clear plastic) and by not allowing light to escape from its walls. The pulses of light bounce along the fibre by a series of total internal reflections. This process is similar to the way jets of water in illuminated fountains trap the light from underwater light sources, and then release it as the individual jets disintegrate (the transmission path stops).

Today's fibres are about 0.1 mm in diameter, with a central light-transmitting core of silica glass of about half that diameter. The rest of the fibre is cladding and filling, to aid transmission and to provide protection for the core. Several such fibres may be laid alongside to form an optical-fibre waveguide or cable, as shown in Fig. 5.2. Fibres and

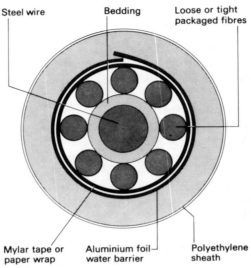

Fig. 5.2 Optical-fibre cable in cross-section (British Telecom)

Steel wire

Bedding

Loose or tight packaged fibres

Mylar tape or paper wrap

Aluminium foil water barrier

Polyethylene sheath

cables are light-weight, flexible, and of high strength. The bandwidth of an optical cable is greater than that of a metal coaxial cable. Data transmitted at the rate of about 140 million bit/s can be sent almost without distortion in an optical cable over about 8 km. A coaxial cable, at the same data rate, would produce unacceptable distortion after only a few kilometres. Current research is aiming at increasing the range of transmission to 50–100 km, before regeneration is required, and at increasing the data-transmission rate.

Example of an optical link

In Britain, the first optical-fibre communication link came into public use on 8 September 1980. It was the first stage of a plan, extending to 1982, to install 450 km of cable in various parts of the country. Figure 5.3 shows the details of this plan, indicating that three different data transmission rates are to be used. The first 9 km link, between Brownhills and Walsall, operates at about 8 million bit/s and can transmit 120 simultaneous telephone calls. The other two speeds, 34 Mbit/s and 140 Mbit/s approximately, correspond to 480 and 1920 two-way telephone circuits respectively. The plan represents a £6m investment.

The new network is able to make use of existing cable ducts and exchange buildings, so installation costs are low. Moreover, optical-fibre cables can resist the ill-effects of sea-water much better than the metal cables of today, and due to their lighter weight can be suspended to form aerial cables in the rugged countryside of Wales, where the laying of ducts would be prohibitively expensive. These costs savings are offset, to some extent, by the cost of the cable itself and of the conversion equipment between optical and electronic signals.

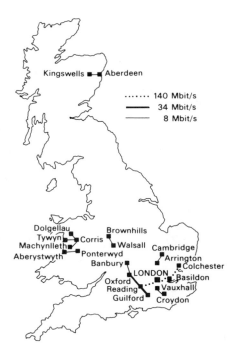

Fig. 5.3 Optical-fibre telecommunication link in Britain, planned for 1982, uses three different transmission rates. (Source: *Post Office Research Review 1979*)

Applications

The primary field of applications of optical communication systems is telecommunications, but it has potential uses wherever wires and cables are employed at the present time. In telecommunications, optical-fibre cables are well suited to the new range of computer-controlled telephone exchanges, to form a completely new all-digital data network (see p. 115). This will handle both speech and computer data in the form of pulses rather than as a continuous electrical signal, as in the present system. The advantage of such a mode of transmission is a better quality service, as digital transmission is less susceptible to interference. The optical-fibre cable contributes to this better performance by using a non-electrical mode of transmission, which leaves it unaffected by electromagnetic disturbances (induced voltages, clicks, atmospheric effects, etc.).

The high-bit-rate cables are currently economical only where the capacity of the cables is fully utilized, as in inter-city trunk routes and submarine cables. They are in competition, however, with radio and satellite transmission systems. But the bandwidth of even the lower-bit-rate optical-fibre cables makes them attractive as a possible alternative or supplement to the wire-pairs used in local networks (taking the telephone service to subscribers—see p. 59). A wide-band optical cable could supply not only the voice-grade service of the present but also the video services envisaged for the future: view-phone (Picturephone), videotex, advanced facsimile, etc. It can also fulfil, in a single entity, the role of present cable-tv installations.

Due to the cost involved, it is unlikely that the present metal wires and cables into homes and offices will be replaced by optical-fibre cables in the near future. Any such move is likely to occur over an extended period of time: first in applications where the wide-band services are sufficiently important to justify an extra cost. Later, optical-fibre cables may be used in all new installations and where the connection is in need of renewal. An example of this step-by-step approach is a 17 km optical-fibre link for British Rail due to come into operation in 1981. It is aimed at modernizing the railways' signalling system and bringing it up to full international standards. Another example, aimed at demonstrating future possibilities, is the installation of an optical-fibre network to replace local telephone wires for 5000 subscribers in the Biarritz area of France. Apart from improved telephone communications, the promise here is added services: tv and vhf radio, data and facsimile links using the same transmission medium, rather than requiring individual wiring.

Apart from telecommunication applications, optical fibres are also used for transmitting signals in aircraft, in measuring instruments, in high-voltage installations, etc., where their strength lies in their being unaffected by extraneous electromagnetic 'noise' and so providing more reliable transmission.

An important feature of optical-fibre cables in such applications is the difficulty of tapping them. This results in more secure data transfer than with metal cables, because any attempt to interfere with optical transmission causes an immediate change in the received signal, which is easily detected.

Local networks may use optical communication without resorting to fibres for transmission. Signals may be carried over short distances by infrared light. One such system, developed by IBM in Switzerland, consists of a source–receiver mounted on the ceiling of a large office, with corresponding source–receivers at each work-station in the office. The system can be used to link each work-station to a larger telecommunication or data network. The advantage it offers over wires is that it does not need re-connecting when the layout of the office is changed or when the work-stations are replaced by equipment requiring a higher bandwidth link.

Another interesting application of direct optical transmission is its use as a secondary or back-up channel in an existing telecommunication network. For example, British Telecom is to set up such a secondary network in the City of London. It will be based on infrared lasers mounted on roof-tops.

Optical communication is one of the major growth areas in the engineering substructure of information technology. With anticipated developments in optical sensor, switching and display technologies, it offers a wide-band, light-weight, low-cost and safe alternative to metal-cable networks.

Further reading

Miller, S. E. and Chynoweth, A. G. (ed.). (1979). *Optical Fiber Telecommunications,* Academic Press.

Sandbank, C. P. (ed.). (1980). *Optical Fibre Communication Systems,* Wiley.

6 Video-tape and video-disc systems

Introduction and fundamentals

Video tape and disc are *signal-storage media*. Used in conjunction with replay equipment and a video display unit, they can reproduce recorded pictures and sound. With appropriate equipment, users can record their own material on video tape; video discs at the present time are primarily replay-only media. Both can be used for the storage and retrieval of computer-coded data, as well as of television signals.

Video tape and disc systems have been developed, from the late 1950s, for the recording and subsequent display of television images and sound. Historically, video tape was the first to be exploited for this purpose, by the Ampex Corporation, which still hold the original patents. Sony of Japan showed the possibility of recording video by the 'helical scan' method, with Philips leading the way to the video-cassette tape (commercially available first in 1972).

In theory, the recording and replaying of tv pictures are simple processes. There must be a sufficiently detailed representation made of the pictures on the recording medium (about half a million picture points per frame), and this must be replayed at a speed sufficient to give the impression of natural movement between each frame (there are 25 frames/s in the European standard, and 30 frames/s in the US standard). The television picture is produced by a process of scanning each frame by a beam of electrons. The variations in the details of the picture are transformed into a coded signal for transmission and/or recording. The bandwidth of this signal is about 5.5 MHz, some 350 times greater than the 15 kHz bandwidth of audio transmission/recording.

In practice, the ability of a recording–replay machine to cope with this bandwidth depends on the relative speed of motion of the recording medium and the signal converter, or 'head', in the machine. In a video-tape recorder, the medium (tape) moves rather slowly (at a few centimetres per second) past an array of rapidly rotating heads (1500–1800 rev/min). In a video-disc player, the head moves slowly across a rapidly rotating disc. Beyond these simple principles, there lies a confusing range of implementations. Apart from the variety of methods used by different manufacturers to produce high-quality images and sound in a reliable, low-cost system, there are also national differences in the way television pictures are produced in the first place.

The United States was first to introduce colour television in 1954. The National Television System Committee (NTSC) standard, still in use there and in Japan, uses 30 frames/s and 525 lines of scan per frame. Due to the way it encodes colour data, it is prone to errors in the true reproduction of colour. To improve on this, two new tv standards were introduced in Europe in 1967:

(a) The Pal (*phase alternation line*) system, used in most of Europe, in Australia, and many countries of Africa and the Far East;

(b) the Secam (*sequential couleur à memoire*) system, used in France, the USSR, East Germany, and many Middle Eastern countries.

Pal is in many ways similar to NTSC, but uses 25 frames/s, 625 lines/frame and codes colour data differently. Secam is totally incompatible with either of the other systems. In spite of this, the original division persists, due to the large investments already made in studio equipment and receivers. So, any recording and playback system for tv signals must follow one or another, or several of these standards, and thus be either incompatible or costly. These problems, from the users' point of view, are compounded by the differences between the various manufacturers' products, which are best seen by examining video tape and disc systems separately.

Video-cassette tape systems

There are two main types of cassette system: that intended for the large-volume consumer entertainment market, and that for the higher-cost, professional applications. Philips' V2000, VHS and Beta are examples of the former, and Sony's U-Matic is now the virtually only representative of the latter.

One difference between the two types is that consumer systems use $\frac{1}{2}$ in wide tape, professional systems $\frac{3}{4}$ in and 1 in tape. On both, the video signals are recorded in adjacent tracks at an angle across the tape, as shown diagrammatically in Fig. 6.1. Sound is recorded as a separate

Fig. 6.1 Video tape track layout. The video data are laid down as continuous 'tracks' of magnetization. Since the head moves across the tape, and the tape moves as shown, the tracks are at an angle. This makes good use of the available recording surface. The control track ensures that during replay the head follows the same path as during recording

(Source: *From television to home computer*, A. Robertson (Ed.), Blandford, 1979)

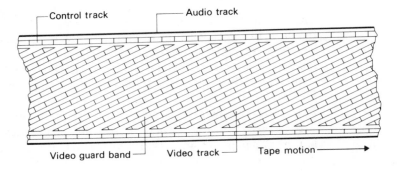

track, along the length of the tape, in the usual way. Another length-wise track controls the position of the heads during replay, to ensure that they are precisely aligned with the tracks.

The various manufacturers' systems differ mainly in the way the tape is wound on the cassette spools, and in the path the tape follows in relation to the rotating drum which carries the record/replay heads. Figure 6.2(a), (b) shows the Philips VCR-LP system, Fig. 6.3(a), (b) the VHS (Video Home System) format, and Fig. 6.4 the Beta format. In each case, although the threading of the tape is automatic, the operation is dependent on a high-precision, complex electromechanical system. Other drawbacks include the wear-out of heads, after about 1000 h use. In the VCR and Beta systems, the tape is pressed against the head drum as soon as the power is on, so that if the tape is not started within a few minutes

Fig. 6.2 Video-cassette formats: Philips N1700—(a) unthreaded tape; (b) threaded tape

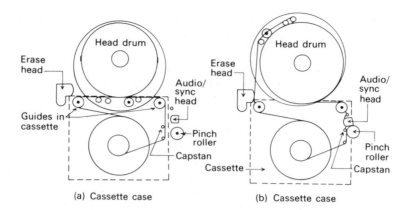

Fig. 6.3 Video-cassette formats: VHS—(a) unthreaded tape; (b) threaded tape

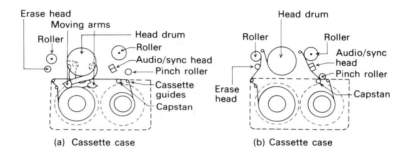

Fig. 6.4 Video-cassette formats: Beta—threaded tape

(Source: *From television to home computer*, A. Robertson (Ed.), Blandford, 1979)

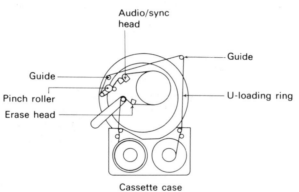

the tape may also get badly worn. These problems are the subject of intense research, and the technology of video-tape systems is undergoing rapid development. For example, the most recent range of video recorders includes features like freeze-frame, slow motion, fast motion and rapid search for individual frames.

Turning now to video-tape systems for professional use, the U-Matic system was introduced by Sony in 1972. From the start, the U-Matic machines have catered for both the Pal and NTSC systems simultaneously; some of the later models also included an ability to replay U-Matic format tapes on Secam-standard receivers. The U-Matic system produces a high-quality picture, can incorporate electronic editing facilities for program production, and is available in battery-operated, portable units.

Video-disc systems

As noted earlier, in video-disc systems it is the medium (the disc) that rotates fast, rather than the head. The necessary bandwidth can be achieved by rotating the disc at 1500 rev/min (for 25 frames/s operation). Alternatively, the disc may rotate more slowly (about 500 rev/min) but with the signals more densely 'packed' than on the faster-rotating disc. The advantage of the higher speeds is that at 1500 or 1800 rev/min a full picture frame is recorded per revolution. Consequently, a freeze-frame or still-picture effect can be achieved by simply halting the movement of the head across the disc. The slower speed has the advantage of longer playing time per disc.

As with video-cassette tape systems, there are several incompatible video-disc standards on the market. The differences lie in the physical principles employed at the recording and replay stages, the size and material of the disc, and the optional facilities provided.

Video high-density format

The video high-density format (vhd) was introduced by the Japanese Victor Company (JVC) in 1978 and has since found backers in Matsushita (Japan), Thorn–EMI (UK) and General Electric (USA). The principles of operation are illustrated in Fig. 6.5. The disc is 254 mm

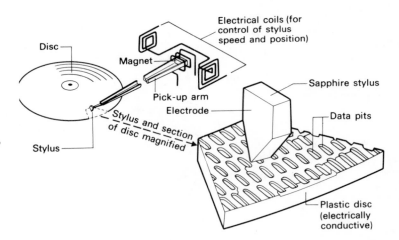

Fig. 6.5 The VHD video-disc system. The magnified section on the right shows the data pits which carry the message and the control signals

(Source: *From television to home computer*, A. Robertson (Ed.), Blandford, 1979)

(10 in) in diameter and is made of an electrically conductive plastic. Data are coded in the form of changes in electrical capacitance. The tiny capacitors are formed by microscopic pits in the surface of the disc. The pits are arranged as a spiral track, with adjacent tracks 1.35 µm apart. (This is about 1/40th of the width of a human hair. By comparison, the grooves on a 78 rev/min audio disc are 150 µm apart.) Apart from the data pits, a second set of pits is used to guide the pick-up stylus, or head.

The head is not guided mechanically by the tracks, as with an audio disc. Indeed, the surface of the disc is smooth. The position of the head is determined by an electronic control system using the data supplied by the tracking pits. The pits are originally formed by a high-energy laser in a glass master disc. The instantaneous intensity of the laser is determined by the video–audio signal to be recorded. The master disc is then used to produce plastic pressings. The production cost of the master may be several hundred dollars, but that of the plastic disc only pennies, in commercial quantities.

The disc rotates at 750 rev/min and carries 2 h of program material—1 h on each side. This corresponds to 90 000 frames per side (NTSC). An add-on feature is a frame-search facility which gives random access to any frame on either side in seconds. This makes the disc equivalent to a 180 000 page 'book', with about 2000 characters per page. Another add-on feature is high-density audio (ahd), which converts the disc system to a digital-audio replay machine.

Against this, the low rotational speed of the vhd disc means that there are *two* frames recorded for each turn of the disc. This makes the freezing of single frames difficult, particularly when the two frames in the same groove are different. Also, this system is very sensitive to contamination of the surface of the disc and requires that the disc be kept in a protective sleeve, or 'caddie', at all times.

SelectaVision

This system, by RCA, is also based on capacitance-coded signals. This time, however, the metallized, diamond-tipped stylus is guided mechanically by grooves in the disc's surface. The speed of rotation is about 450 rev/min, and a repeat-action facility is available. The current RCA player, however, does not offer random access or hi-fi sound options. The disc has also to be protected permanently from contamination of its surface. Due to the permanent mechanical contact between the disc and the stylus, this system can lead to the wear-out of both. The relatively low speed of rotation implies that this time there are *four* recorded frames per revolution of the disc, making a freeze-frame facility very difficult to achieve.

Laservision

The third main system, developed by Philips, works on a completely different principle. A plastic, 305 mm (12 in) disc is coated by a reflecting silvery metallized layer. The video data are carried by a pitted spiral track, as shown in Fig. 6.6. The head contains a tiny laser, the light from which is reflected back from the disc to the head. A sensor there picks up the variations in the reflected light caused by the pits, and generates an electrical signal which represents the recorded data. The playing time of each side of the disc is 1 h, but with an add-on option, a random-access facility to any frame on the disc is available. In this case, however, the continuous playing time is reduced to $\frac{1}{2}$ h each side.

Optical systems, such as this, are not sensitive to surface contamination because, just as a dust particle on a camera lens, it is out-of-focus. Also, there is no mechanical contact between head and disc so there is no wear-out. On the debit side, the need for a laser and for a very high accuracy in the positioning of the head imposes considerable demands on the engineering, cost and reliability of the system.

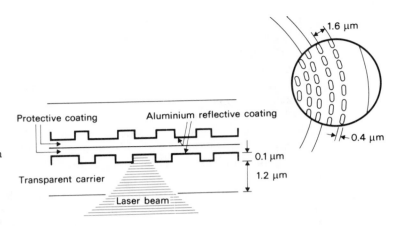

Fig. 6.6 The Laservision video-disc system. The diagram on the left shows the disc in cross-section. The magnified area on the right is a top view, showing the pits whose presence or absence carries the message. The disc is re-played by detecting the reflection of laser light from the pitted grooves

(Source: *From television to home computer*, A. Robertson (Ed.), Blandford, 1979)

Thomson CSF

This French system also uses a laser as a means of 'reading' the disc. This time, the light from the laser passes through, rather than is reflected from, the disc. It is the variations in the intensity of the transmitted light which carry the coded video and audio signals. In a recent development, Thomson have linked up with Xerox to produce a read-only disc for computer-coded data.

The use of video discs for data storage offers the prospect of a low-cost storage medium. Theoretically, the density of data recorded on a video disc can be 100 times higher than on a magnetic disc (an upper limit of 10^{10} bit/cm^2, compared with 10^8 bit/cm^2). However, at the present state of development, video discs cannot be re-used once a particular data pattern has been recorded on them, whereas the magnetic disc is re-usable.

Applications

The main applications areas of video-tape and disc systems at present are in the home, for entertainment and education, in commerce and industry as a means of presentation, advertising and training, and in the information industry as a means of electronic publishing and electronic news gathering. This latter application requires a video-tape system, since recording on video discs is still a complex and costly process. There are, however, some developments which promise progress in this area: the magnetic disc used by broadcasting organizations has been adapted to produce a lower-cost version, and discs employing light transmission have been recorded, as well as replayed, using a laser as part of the equipment supplied to the user.

The range of applications of both tape and disc systems depends also on the availability and perceived value of program material. With the diversity of incompatible systems on the market, this factor currently favours video-tape systems: broadcast material can be recorded on any tape machine. A disc player, however, is unable to record 'off-air' and can only play compatible discs. Each disc system, therefore, has to develop its own program 'library' separately. Against this, the video disc offers a generally much higher picture and sound quality and, on some systems, rapid access to any frame, or sequence of frames, on the disc. Its ability to give a high-quality reproduction of a single frame, combined with the freedom to move from that frame to any one of a set of logically linked frames makes the disc of particular interest in educational, training and retailing applications.

The cost factor is also in favour of the disc: disc replay machines currently cost less than tape machines, primarily because of the greater mechanical complexity of the latter. The disc is also cheaper as a distribution medium for program material: full-length feature films (the only current means of comparison) on disc are about one-third of the price of the same films on cassette. This ratio is, of course, sensitive to the volume of production and sales, and to advances in technology and standardization.

Further reading

Robertson, A. (ed.) (1979). *From Television to Home Computer*, Blandford Press.

7 Computers

Introduction

In the context of information technology, computers take on the role of *automatic data processors*. The processing operations which they can perform on data are limited only by the demands of complete and unambiguous specification of the task—at least in theory. In practice, these demands are often difficult, if not impracticable, to fulfil, as in the case of tasks modelling human intelligence (e.g. expert systems—see p. 91). In other cases, the capacity and performance of computer equipment prove to be the limiting factor, although continuing advances in fields like data networks (see p. 107), voice input and output (see p. 101), and computer vision (see p. 83) keep pushing these limits further and further back. Yet other practical constraints on computers include cost, reliability, physical size—again, these have become less significant in the last few years, with advances in microelectronics. In the final count, therefore, the use of computers by information technology is likely to be determined by the extent to which people find tools based on them helpful and acceptable.

Within the space available, this chapter can give only a broad overview of these theoretical and practical considerations. For a more detailed understanding of specific aspects, the reader is urged to turn to sources such as those listed in Further Reading.

What is an automatic data processor?

Computers deal with representations of information rather than with information itself (the distinction between information and its representation was discussed in Chapter 1). The representations which a computer can manipulate and communicate are a form of *data*. In the context of information technology, data can include a variety of formalized representations (speech, handwriting, physical measurements, etc.) but the most widely used type of computer, the electronic digital computer, employs only *digital representations*. As described in Chapter 1, 'digital' does not only relate to digits, or numbers, but includes any finite set of symbols or characters. So, digital data can take the form of letters of an alphabet, or words of a natural language made up of those letters, or speech coded into numbers or symbols, or results of measurement expressed by a finite sequence of digits, etc.

The reason behind this requirement of digital data lies in the engineering aspects of electronic computers: they can only manipulate digital signals. Indeed, within the computer, the digital signals must be of a special kind: binary signals with only two possible values—on or off, or pulse or no-pulse. (An item of digital data or digital signal represented by a 1 or a 0 is called a *bit*, short for *binary digit*.) Computers use binary signals because low-cost electronic circuits are available for their fast, reliable, accurate processing and storage.

But the real world does not often oblige the computer with digital data, let alone with binary ones. So, the computer usually includes devices for converting real-life data into the binary representation of the computer, and back again into an appropriate form. In between the two conversions, the data can be simply stored for later use, or it may be subjected to some processing operations. The simplest graphical representation of a computer therefore includes four interlinked boxes, as shown in Fig. 7.1.

Fig. 7.1 The simplest model of a computer consists of a data processor linked to devices for storing and converting data. The data conversion necessary between the internal and external representations of information is carried out by the input and output devices

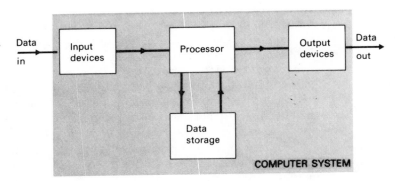

The *input devices* can take the form of a keyboard, or a digitizer for graphics or speech, or some other data converter. The *processor* is an assembly of electronic circuits. The *memory*, or *store*, can employ electronic, magnetic or optical media. *Output devices* again may be chosen from a variety of data conversion units, such as printers, visual displays, voice output devices. Input and output devices may also include links to other computers and to data networks, for the direct transfer of digital data. The devices making up a computer are referred to collectively as the *hardware*.

The hardware may appear, in some cases, to be able to perform certain tasks *automatically*, that is without any routine human intervention. For example, a computer on board a space ship, or even in some cars, takes in data, works out settings, displays results completely automatically. However, what is happening is that the computer follows a routine which has been worked out for it in advance and stored in its memory. The routine consists of a sequence of steps, or elementary operations, which completely define the task in hand, be it as complex as the navigation of a space module, or as simple as the calculation of the fuel consumption of a car. The prime requirement, however, is that the prescription of what the computer is to do with the data is to be complete and unambiguous. Complete in the sense that it deals with all eventualities that may occur during the performance of the task, and unambiguous in the sense that for any eventuality the required action is uniquely defined.

The prescription itself must be expressed in a form and in a representation which the processor is equipped to interpret. Built into the circuitry of the processor is a finite set of elementary operations which it can perform on given data. These will include, as a rule

(a) mathematical, logical, comparison and other *processing operations*;
(b) *storage operations*, for storing and retrieving specified items of data;
(c) *input* and *output operations* which accept data from input devices and send data to output devices, in a specified format;
(d) *control operations*, which organize the order or sequencing of other operations.

These operations are each invoked by specific codes, which activate appropriate circuits of the processor. The operation codes, together with the relevant data, form the *instructions* to the computer. A sequence of instructions to accomplish a specific task is known as a *program*. The collection of programs prepared for a computer is called its *software*.

The power and versatility of the computer derive from the way its hardware and software combine in the processing of data. The hardware contributes a variety of possible processing operations which have been designed so as to make the computer a *general-purpose data processor*. That is, a program can be constructed to accomplish *any* completely and unambiguously defined task. What the software does is to select a sequence of these operations which convert the computer to a *special-purpose processor* for the duration of the program's working.

The hardware also contributes speed of operation and memory. Once a program has been worked out, it can be stored as a form of data in the computer's memory. The processor can then be made to perform this program by a single instruction from its operator, *at its own speed*. Present-day computers operate at speeds of up to 30 million instructions *per second*. So, highly complex and lengthy programs, which may have taken a team of specialists years to develop can be performed in a small fraction of that time, repeatedly and repeatably.

The assumption here, though, is that the program is complete, that is, that all the data required to accomplish a task are already stored inside the computer. In many cases, however, some of the data will be produced outside the computer while the program is in operation. These cases are called, in computer jargon, *real-time* tasks. They include interactive uses of the computer, such as the monitoring and control of other equipment, text preparation, computer-assisted learning. In these situations, the computer still operates at its own fast speed on the data at its disposal, then waits for the new data to arrive so that the program can be resumed. If the waiting time is a significant proportion of the total time, the computer may be able to handle more than one task, yet give full service to each of them. This mode of operation is described as *time-sharing*.

So, we see the computer as a combination of electronic and other devices (hardware) and programs (software). The programs prescribe, in complete detail, the operations which the hardware is to perform upon suitably coded data. The programs are stored in the computer, again as suitably coded data. When a program is started off, the processing is carried out automatically, at high speed and with great precision. In this sense, the computer is an automatic data processor. But whether a computer is the right tool in an information technology application depends on practical considerations; to these we turn next.

Computer software Computer software is of two kinds: system software and application software.

System software

System software is produced to improve the general usability of the computer, rather than to cope with particular applications. Without system software, the detailed control of the computer's operation and the preparation of application programs would be rather tedious. The tasks performed by system software include the translation of the operator's commands from a near-natural language to the elementary instructions for the processor. They assist people in the editing, testing, modification and storage of new programs, in the rapid re-allocation of hardware resources in the time-sharing mode, in maintaining files of data and making them available as required by user programs, etc.

System software is usually supplied ready-made, rather than having to be produced by each user of a computer. However, a particular item of system software is unlikely to work in computers of other manufacturers. The reason for this is that different makes of computer tend to use somewhat different sets of elementary instructions from which the programs are built up, as well as different codes for specifying these instructions. There have been attempts to standardize at least those items of system software which help users to create new application programs in near-natural computer languages. Computer languages (allowed symbols and rules for their use) such as Cobol, Basic, Pascal, Fortran which are widely used around the world, have unfortunately their 'dialects', or minor variations, which prevent the wide-scale interchange of programs expressed in them. These dialects are not geographically related, though, but rather differ from manufacturer to manufacturer, each of whom claims some advantage for the variants specific to them.

Application software

As a result of the existence of these dialects, the production of application programs still tends to be a relatively small-scale, highly labour-intensive activity, which is reflected in the high cost of software. This is not only due to the lack of standardization of languages. Economies of scale are difficult to achieve in adapting the general-purpose computer to specific tasks when the detailed requirements vary from user to user, from situation to situation. The only viable alternatives open to would-be users are to produce or commission the production of custom-made application programs, or else to adapt their specific requirements to the programs which may already exist for a particular make of computer.

The recent emergence of microcomputers brought some relief to this dilemma: certain makes of microprocessor have achieved sufficient sales to stimulate the production of a wide range of off-the-peg application packages. Many of these packages are aimed at the fairly predictable requirements of business applications (e.g. text processing, payroll, inventory), research applications (e.g. mathematical and design problems), or hobbyist uses (e.g. graphics, games, money management) in fields where microcomputers enjoy large sales. General-purpose software packages called *program generators* are being marketed to reduce even further the laborious task of translating (coding) a program specification into the language of the computer. These do not, however, eliminate the crucial stage of specifying the task to be performed by the application program completely and unambiguously.

The lack of availability of high-quality, reliable, low-cost, well-documented software packages to fit all makes of computer is likely to remain a stumbling block in information technology (as well as other application areas of computers) for years to come.

Computer hardware

The lack of standardization in the computer field afflicts hardware just as much as it does software. A processor developed by a particular manufacturer can work only with the input, output and memory devices which are compatible with it—usually a small fraction of such products on the market. There is also rapid progress in hardware technology so that products are quickly outdated. For example, in the early 1970s a powerful processor, capable of operating in the time-sharing mode with 16 users, cost about $50 000. It needed a great deal of additional equipment to offer such a service, including 16 input–output terminals, such as video terminals. In the early 1980s a processor, equivalent in power, is available for about $3000. Moreover, it has been reduced in size to the extent that each video terminal can contain its own processor and no time-sharing is necessary. Instead, the terminal can include functions hitherto provided by specialized devices—memory units, telecommunication interfaces, etc., although some of the more expensive devices—disc files, printers, etc.—may still be shared with other users' terminals.

This trend towards including all the major hardware components of a computer in a single box of the size of a television set is leading to a reduction of some of the compatibility problems, by reducing the number of separate boxes to be interconnected. However, for the time being, computer hardware needs to be considered under the separate headings of processor, data storage, input and output units.

Processors

Processors are often grouped into three categories, on the basis of their physical size: *microprocessors* (single integrated circuits, or chips), *minicomputers* (usually larger arrays of integrated circuits), and *main-frames* (large cabinets full of electronic circuits). The progression in size also corresponds to a progression in cost and speed of operation. There is, however, no difference in the principles (data representations, storage and processing methods, interfacing with other equipment, etc.) which govern the design of the three different types of processor.

A great deal of research and development work is going into the design of new types of processor which are more suited to specific information handling tasks, rather than being general-purpose, as today's processors are. For example, processors for data-base operations, for content-related search and data retrieval, for simultaneous, rather than sequential steps in program operation, are being built and evaluated.

Data storage

There is also rapid progress in data-storage technology, in which a variety of physical effects is being exploited for the temporary or long-term storage of binary-coded data. Semiconductor-based storage devices include *random-access memory* (ram) and *read-only memory* (rom) integrated circuits. The first of these types can be used to store *or* retrieve data, under the control of the processor. The second type has data permanently or semi-permanently 'built' into it, and can be only interrogated by the processor.

The trend towards more and more complex processor and memory components packed into smaller and smaller circuits is illustrated in Fig. 7.2. At the time of writing, the 'state-of-the-art' in very large-scale

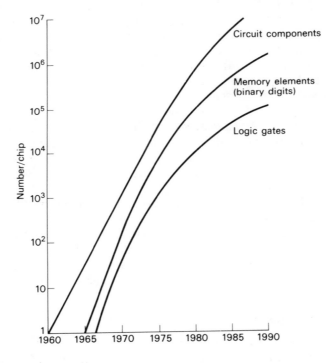

Fig. 7.2 The number of various types of electronic circuit constructed on a single chip, projected to 1990. (Source: *Report of the Committee on Data Protection*, HM Stationery Office, 1979)

integration (vlsi) is the 32-bit microprocessor containing about 225 000 semiconductor elements in an area about 5 cm (2 in) square. To gain an idea of the fineness of detail necessary to produce the circuit elements on the chip, imagine a map of the British Isles showing sufficient detail to identify even the narrowest side-street in London. At the currently achievable line thickness in integrated circuits, the entire map could be reproduced within the 5 cm square area of the 32-bit microprocessor.

Storage components also show a similar trend, as illustrated in Fig. 7.3. The current 64 kbit solid-state random access memories are

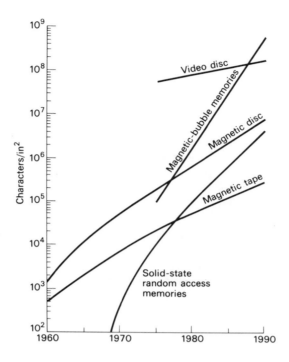

Fig. 7.3 Projections of the data-storage densities of various media. The units of characters/in^2 may be converted to bits/cm^2 by multiplying each value along the vertical axis by 50. (Source: *Report of the Committee on Data Protection*, HM Stationery Office, 1979)

expected to be soon superseded by 256 kbit ones, capable of storing 262 144 bits of data on a chip measuring 5 mm by 9 mm. An even higher density storage medium was announced in 1981. A credit-card size of plastic coated with a new organic film can hold about 40 million bits of data. This storage medium, with the trade name Drexon, can thus accommodate some 5 million text characters, sufficient to fill about 10 average-sized books.

Magnetic storage media include *magnetic tape* and *disc* devices and *magnetic bubble* devices. Tape and disc are able to store and present large quantities of data under the control of the processor (they are often called mass-storage devices). Tape units include cassette and reel-to-reel types, while discs are available either in flexible ('floppy disc') or rigid (fixed-head or moving-head) form. Magnetic bubble devices first became available in 1977 and are still the subject of intensive development. At the time of writing, they are more comparable, in terms of their storage capacity, with the faster-acting but lower-capacity semiconductor memory devices than the other magnetic storage media.

In addition to semiconductor and magnetic memory devices, *optical-storage technology* is also coming to the fore. *Microforms* (see p. 95) are being used in two modes: either to store data in direct text or graphic form, readable by people or by machines, or as *holograms* which require laser-based recording and reading apparatus. At the present stage of technology, a micro-fiche can store, as holograms, about as much data as the lowest-capacity magnetic tape and disc devices. However, magnetic storage is easily erased and over-written, while optical media are usually of the read-only (permanent or semi-permanent) type.

Data input and output

Data input is currently dominated by keyboard devices. Keyboards are being used for coding text from teletypewriters, video terminals, key-to-disc units, etc., into a form (digital signals) used by the processor. There is, however, an increasing range of other devices to convert data to this form: optical and magnetic document (character) readers, laser scanners, graphic tablets and digitizers, voice input devices, analogue-to-digital converters, telecommunication modems, etc.

Data-output devices fall into four main categories: display, voice, hard-copy, and digital signal outputs. Display devices are based mainly on the cathode-ray, or television, tube but other light-emitting or reflecting devices (e.g. plasma, liquid-crystals) are also in use. Voice output is considered on p. 101. 'Hard-copy' is a term usually applied to output on paper or photographic film. It can be produced by printers of various types (impact, thermal, ink-jet, electrostatic laser and other forms), plotters (primarily for graphical output) and special cameras (e.g. computer-output microfilm equipment). Digital signals can be a useful form of output when connecting to or controlling other pieces of equipment, e.g. via the telephone network, or directly linked to switches and other actuators.

Further reading

Cassel, D. and Jackson, M. (1980). *Introduction to Computers and Information Processing*, Prentice-Hall.
Fry, T. F. (1978). *Beginner's Guide to Computers*, Newnes.

8 Computer vision

Introduction

'Computer vision' is a term applied, in the first instance, to the input of images into computer-based systems. The term is often extended to include the processing (enhancement, interpretation, 'perception', etc.) of images. Work in this field is largely at the research and development stage. It links closely with work on artificial intelligence (expert systems—see p. 91) and voice communication with computers (see p. 101).

Considering computer vision in its wider sense, there are three distinct processes in evidence in the majority of working systems:

(a) input, or image acquisition;
(b) processing, or analysis of the data;
(c) output, or interfacing the system to a human or machine user.

Image input

The input of images is handled by specialized sensors. These may be a video scanner (a form of television camera), or an array of photodetectors. Both types of device convert the intensity of light representing an image into electronic signals. The representation, just as in the eye, is only a limited part of the visual world at any one time. Early work was mainly concerned with two-dimensional images, derived from a single sensor. More recently, work has concentrated on three-dimensional views, which require several, coordinated sensors.

The image is 'handed over' from the input to the processing stage as an array or grid of picture elements, often abbreviated as *pixels*. Each pixel represents the intensity, and in some systems the colour, of a small part of the image.

Image processing

The processing of the array of picture elements is in most systems based on the assumption that the original image is made up of one or more objects. These may be objects in the usual sense of the word (such as parts which an industrial robot has to assemble or unknown structures on the surface of a distant planet), or they may be finger-prints or handwritten characters, etc. The processing stage then consists of three steps:

1 segmentation, or breakdown of the image into the objects contained in it;
2 recognition, or 'naming' of each object;
3 interpretation, or the analysis of the interrelations among objects.

There is a similarity of approach here to the processing of speech by computers (see p. 102) to the extent that it is usually referred to as the *linguistic approach* to computer vision.

Segmentation

In the segmentation process, objects are frequently characterized by their outlines or overall shape, as this represents a reduction of the amount of data that needs to be handled during processing. (The processing stages, particularly of complex, rapidly changing images, put a sometimes impossible burden on the present generation of computers.) In some cases, additional features, like the texture or surface properties of objects, are included in their overall descriptions.

Recognition

During recognition, the computer's task is to match certain features of each object to a stored set of patterns or templates. It is the choice of the features used for recognition that is perhaps the most important distinction between the various systems employing the linguistic approach. The choice of features is indeed a crucial one since they must be efficient in distinguishing objects from one another, few in number to speed up processing, and invariant to changes in position, orientation and size of the object, and to minor errors in its representation. After all, a letter A, for example, must be identified as such, irrespective of where it occurs or who writes it.

Interpretation

The interpretation process involves the complete image. It is equivalent to building up a descriptive sentence from a set of words. This process is necessary in the analysis of complex scenes, and it is also helpful in identifying those objects which were missed at the recognition stage, from information supplied by the context.

Other methods

Variants of the approach just described include those which start the processing by looking at the overall image and then proceed to specific objects or sub-areas rather than the other way round. Computer-vision systems also differ in the relative extent of processing performed by software and by hardware. Programmed systems are more convenient to modify, which is an asset in the development process. Hardware implementations are faster and can perform a number of different processes simultaneously. The output stage of computer vision is governed by the use to which the system is put. An automatic reading machine, for example, would produce an output as it processes each character, but an automatic surveillance system would generate a response only after identifying changes in the scene under observation. An industrial inspection machine would alert its operator only when it detects an out-of-the-ordinary image.

Applications

Computer-vision systems in current production, as opposed to those in the research stage, are aimed at applications where the images are two-dimensional and made up of isolated objects. These include certain industrial automation systems, where the vision system identifies components as they arrive on a conveyor belt or in a component bin. A robot arm then manipulates the components according to the requirements of the task. In other industrial automation systems, the vision system has been used for parts inspection, materials handling and simple assembly tasks.

Commercially available systems also can deal with printed text, and some with certain forms of handwritten text. Laboratory systems have been used to handle, among other things, images of finger-prints, aerial photographs, and magnified views of microelectronic circuits.

Current research is concentrated on ways of dealing with three-dimensional images, from arbitrary viewpoints and lighting conditions. More general problems include dealing with images of non-rigid objects, unknown objects and complex scenes at processing speeds matched to real-life situations.

Further reading

Dodd, G. G. and Rossol, L. (1978). *Computer Vision and Sensor-Based Robots*, Plenum.

Hanson, A. R. and Riseman, E. M. (1978). *Computer Vision Systems*, Academic Press.

9 Data protection

Introduction

The increasing use of computers and sophisticated information technology, while essential to the efficient operations of government, has greatly magnified the harm to individual privacy that can occur from any collection, maintenance, use or dissemination of personal information. (From the Preface to the US *Privacy Act*, 1974, Public Law 93–579.)

Data protection is the set of legislative and technical measures taken to ensure the privacy of personal information. The legislative aspects are very much bound up with the notion of 'privacy', and differ from country to country. Thus, legislation in many European countries (Sweden, Denmark, Norway, Luxembourg, West Germany and France) covers the use of data about the individual by both the public and private sectors, and is legally enforcible. In the United States and Canada, it applies only to the public sector and compliance with it is voluntary. In some countries, not only the individual but 'legal persons' (companies, etc.) are also protected by data laws.

Apart from the legislation enacted by various countries, there is also the question of the flow of personal data across national boundaries. Although in May 1981 Britain signed the Council of Europe convention on data protection, it has yet to enact legislation which will bind it to comply with the terms of the convention. Briefly, the convention gives citizens the right to know what records are being stored about them. Those against legislation argue that this would open, in addition to personal and business information, public access to military and security information. It is likely, however, that countries which have enacted the convention will restrict trans-border flow of data to only those countries which have similarly enacted appropriate data protection laws. Otherwise, they argue, 'data havens' may emerge where personal data can be sent (and processed there, with implications for employment in data processing), without it being accessible to public scrutiny. Private data networks operated by banks and multinational corporations, data-bases accessible via public and private telecommunication networks all pose potential threats to privacy. Of the countries mentioned above, the USA and Canada impose no rules on the import and export of data; the others require licencing of data exportation. Some other countries, including Britain, are considering their position on both national and trans-border data protection.

The problems of formulating fair and enforcible data protection laws are formidable. Some of the problems go back to the difficulty of attributing ownership of information (see p. 11). In other words, the privateness of information is not one of its basic characteristics, but rather is dependent on the circumstances in which it has been obtained or given. Individuals may agree to part with information freely, but may wish to restrict the use of it for particular purposes. The report of the Lindop Committee (*Report of the Committee on Data Protection*, 1978, Cmnd 7341, HM Stationery Office) balances this desire with 'the interests of the rest of society, which include the efficient conduct of industry, commerce and administration' (see p. 11 of *Report*).

Other problems have their origin in the technical developments in the storage and handling of data, which entrust personal information to automatic equipment. This raises the question of security of data in computers and telecommunication systems.

Privacy and security

It is important to distinguish between the *privacy* and *security* aspects of data protection. Privacy is concerned with avoiding the misuse of information relating to people or corporate bodies. In practice, it is expressed by laws, principles or codes of practice. Security is concerned with the implementation of these expressions of privacy. Without security, privacy cannot be ensured, but even with security, privacy cannot be guaranteed.

The advent of information technology has not created the problems of privacy and security of information. Rather it has thrown them in a new light, and provided new means of both protecting and breaching the security of data. Before, the cost of obtaining personal data from manual filing systems was relatively high. Now, with computerized data-bases and vast amounts of data in transit, access to it—authorized and unauthorized—is more practicable. Unauthorized access to data can be accidental or deliberate.

Accidental disclosures may result from a system error (both hardware and software) or a human operational error, such as an authorized user not signalling to the system the end of an access transaction, and leaving the system open to an unauthorized inquiry. *Deliberate unauthorized access* is possible while the data are being processed, stored or transmitted. The methods can include legitimate access to the data-base to obtain unauthorized information, obtaining legitimate access by improper means, theft of storage media, wire-tapping, etc.

Security measures against unauthorized access need to be effective and they also must be *seen* to be effective. Both accidental and deliberate disclosures of confidential information can be countered by administrative measures, such as the control of access by passwords, auditing and monitoring, or technical measures of which the most effective is *privacy transformation*, better known as *cryptography*.

Scrambling and unscrambling

The transformation (scrambling) of data can take place prior to its storage or transmission, and can guard against accidental disclosures and wire-tapping or other electronic 'snooping'. Although no code or cypher has been theoretically proved to be unbreakable, the aim of security measures is to make the cost of breaking them greater than the value of information which they protect.

The scrambling and unscrambling of data are processes which are readily performed by computers, but they are, of course, available also to those who deliberately seek unauthorized access. Moreover, the use of a computer for privacy transformation leaves open the question of how to protect the code (key) used in the scrambling process, as well as the need to convince the non-technical individual of the effectiveness of the method. In spite of the strengths of cryptography, embodied in the publication of the *Data Encryption Standard* in the United States in 1975, these two disadvantages appeared to make it unpopular as a data security measure until recently.

The new development came with the idea of using different keys for the scrambling and the unscrambling of data (the Hellman–Diffie method). Moreover, the method allowed for the scrambling key to be made public. If a directory, similar to the telephone directory, is published listing personal keys it becomes possible for a scrambled message to be sent to anyone, which only the intended recipient can unscramble. (The scrambling and unscrambling keys are mathematically related.)

An alternative use of the same method demonstrates another advantage of privacy transformation—the authentication of messages, also known as an *electronic signature*. It works by reversing the roles of scrambling and unscrambling keys. Suppose, for example, that A wants to send a message to B. He first scrambles it with his own *unscrambling* key. The resulting code is then further scrambled with B's published scrambling key. On receipt, B uses his own unscrambling key, but of course still cannot read the message because of the *double scrambling*. Only by applying A's (and only A's) public key can the message be finally unscrambled and simultaneously the identity of the sender verified. Only A could have sent that specific double-scrambled message, so it carries his electronic signature. Fortunately for ordinary users, the method does not require the scrambling and unscrambling to be done by hand, but rather by special microcomputer-based devices, which can be portable and very rapid in operation. Unfortunately, this entrusts security to a device which can be lost, stolen or become faulty.

A less secure alternative (because it uses a much shorter key) is to issue everyone with just a single personal key they can remember—not necessarily a number, but possibly a combination of letters and/or numbers which are chosen by a person for its private memorability. This is known as the personal identity number, or PIN. Such numbers are already in use for the authorization of electronic funds transfers.

Applications

Other application areas of data security techniques, apart from data-banks and electronic banking and shopping, include electronic mail, the use of computing facilities from remote terminals, satellite communications, defence and police work. Indeed, any use of data transmission and storage is a potential area of application. The magnitude of this area is illustrated by Table 9.1, based on information from the British National Computing Index for December 1977. It lists computer applications by industry, with possible relevance to privacy.

Application	Use	Number of computers in operation
Sales	Statements	2622
	Credit control	1992
	Market research	408
Staff	Wages/salaries	3332
	Personnel records	1005
Other commercial	Banking	2092
	Insurance	772
	Information retrieval	596
Education	Administration	292
Medical	Patient records and statistics	178
Statistics	Survey and statistical data	905
On-line	Reservation systems	55
Other	Computer bureaux	2522
	Total	16771

Table 9.1 Extent of computer applications in the UK according to the British National Computing Index, December 1977. (Source: *Report of the Committee on Data Protection*, 1978, Cmnd 7341, HM Stationery Office)

Further reading

Hoffman, L. J. (ed.) (1980). *Computers and Privacy in the Next Decade*, Academic Press.

Katzan, H. (1974). *Computer Data Security*, Van Nostrand Reinhold.

Katzan, H. (1980). *Multinational Computer Systems*, Van Nostrand Reinhold.

Lindop, Sir Norman (chm) (1978). *Report of the Committee on Data Protection*, Cmnd 7341, HM Stationery Office.

Martin, J. (1973). *Security, Accuracy and Privacy in Computer Systems*, Prentice-Hall.

Privacy Protection Study Commission. (1977). *Personal Privacy in an Information Society*.

10 Expert systems

Introduction and fundamentals

Expert systems are software packages (computer programs—see p. 78) aimed at providing expert 'consultancy' advice and assistance with problem-solving in limited specialist fields of science, engineering, mathematics, medicine, education, etc. These systems are currently at the research/development stage and need considerable computer resources for their operation.

Expert systems represent one of the most advanced facets of information technology, in the sense introduced in Part 1. That is, they aid people in some of the most complex and least understood human information handling tasks: decision-making, problem-solving, diagnosis and learning. They do this by storing a large amount of factual information on a subject area, together with lines of reasoning employed by human experts in that area. Most of this material is supplied to the program at the time that it is written, but it also has facilities for adding to this base of information as it is applied in new situations. The subject expertise is provided initially by interviews and observations of successful practitioners of the subject.

Expert systems represent an attempt to harness, as an intellectual tool, those features of the computer where it excels in the handling of data:

(a) its ability for storing a very large amount of data;
(b) the retention of these data for an arbitrarily long time in a prescribed form;
(c) its ability for making precise calculations and exhaustive searches of stored data at high speed.

Although there is not, as yet, a standard approach to the production and operation of expert systems, most of them work on the principle of guiding the user from some 'current situation' to a goal or solution of a stated problem. For this, the programs can employ either 'brute force' or a more 'intelligent' strategy. The 'brute force' approach amounts to looking up, in its memory, a very large table, which lists all possible contingencies (steps of reasoning, actions, etc.) needed to go from the current situation to the goal. Clearly, this approach is highly intensive of storage space (assuming that such exhaustive information is available in the first place), time and cost. In some cases, such as fault tracing in cars and other equipment, or even in the medical diagnosis of certain conditions, the cost may not be prohibitive. An example of the problems involved in the 'brute force' approach comes from the game of chess. Ideally, one would ask the computer to supply the 'winning line' at any stage in the game. To give this advice, the computer would have to store an astronomically large number of possible positions on the board.

Instead, the programs usually *generate* a limited number of possible 'next moves' and *examine* the implications of following each of these paths in terms of their leading to the eventual goal, or even a local sub-goal. Expert knowledge is effectively stored by the computer as a set of empirical rules which help in selecting plausible paths to the goal and in evaluating the situations which then result. Any situation may suggest a possible action or it may lead to a request for further information. The latter would be the case, for example, if in seeking a medical diagnosis the program would suggest that some specific tests be carried out in order to distinguish among several possible conclusions.

Artificial intelligence

Expert systems form a major area of research in a hybrid field known as *artificial intelligence*, or AI. Artificial intelligence brings together computer scientists and engineers, psychologists, and linguists with workers in various areas of its potential application. Such a convergence of many backgrounds and viewpoints is necessary to grapple with three of the main unsolved problems of expert-systems research:

1 How can the user of such a system communicate the problem to the computer in a natural way (rather than having to fall in with the quirks of the computer)?
2 How should the computer deal with the stated problem?

The second is a fundamental question—it leads to further questions of the internal representation of knowledge, the organization of the selected representation to facilitate the search for a particular item and the addition of new items, and the use of common-sense general rules for reasoning, deduction and problem-solving. These are, of course, the questions that psychologists have been asking themselves in relation to human thinking, planning and learning. One aspect of artificial intelligence research is the mutual benefit that can result from psychological research and work on 'knowledgeable' computers.

3 How can people control and check the operation of an expert system?

This is also a crucial question—if the user is presented only with a recommendation, without knowing the reason for that advice, then the system is not really functioning as an aid, but more like a dictator. On the other hand, if the computer automatically presents all the decision points and subsidiary information used to produce the recommendation, this may be too tedious. The program, therefore, needs to adapt itself to the routine needs of its current user, but have the facilities to give a complete account of its 'reasoning' if that is required.

In addition to these three basic questions, research on expert systems also links to work on computer vision (see p. 83) and speech input and output (see p. 101), as means of acquiring data and providing a response to requests; on data-base design, as ways of organizing and interrogating collections of data; and on the general development of computer systems, as the embodiments of working prototypes.

Applications

One of the earliest expert systems was concerned with organic chemistry: the Dendral system. This originated at Stanford University (USA) in 1965, and is still in use as an aid to finding plausible new molecular structures. The program is based on analytical data and on practical constraints, supplied by the user. A later program in the same field, Simulation and Evaluation of Chemical Syntheses (Secs), is being used in pharmaceutical laboratories for suggesting to chemists new compounds which are chemically sound. Among its achievements is the deduction of eight of the 11 known ways of making a pesticide called Grandisol.

In the field of medicine, the task of the Mycin system is to diagnose blood infections and meningitis infections, and to recommend an appropriate drug. Mycin operates by a set of empirical rules which have an associated degree of confidence or reliability. The rules are 'acquired' by another system, by the following procedure: a diagnosis is presented to a medical expert on the basis of the facts of a specific case. If the expert does not agree with the diagnosis, he is shown the line of reasoning of Mycin, and is led back along the logical chain to the point where he finds a fault. The rule there is either changed or a new one is introduced. The 'consultation' is then repeated, until the expert agrees.

Other medical applications include the diagnosis of internal diseases (Internist, Pittsburgh University) and lung diseases (Puff). In other fields of application, the Prospector system uses geological data to deduce the presence of minerals; Sacon is used to advise on problems in structural engineering. There are also numerous chess-playing systems which are used as a testing ground for ideas on expert systems. An expert system is being developed by British Petroleum with the aim of detecting and correcting faults in the operation of oil production platforms. The AL/X system stores the expertise of the designers and operators of platforms about the underlying causes of failures, so that a repair worker can be guided to these rapidly, starting from a superficial symptom of failure.

A further, rapidly developing area of expert system research is language translation. Computer-aided translation would be of service to, say, the member states of the EEC, the potential readers of Chinese and Japanese technical literature, or the frustrated tourist. The current 'state-of-the-art' is moving from a 'brute force' grammatical breakdown and dictionary search method to the 'intelligent' approach of segmenting text into 'chunks of meaning', which are then translated as a whole. Human expertise is being used to identify, in the first instance, such 'chunks of meaning' in various languages. The 'intelligent' approach is claimed to produce a 95 per cent accuracy in the translation of technical Chinese, in comparison with the 75–80 per cent success rate of the 'brute force' method.

All these systems are essentially research tools, of increasing sophistication. There are also some commercially available systems which make use of some of the better-established features of laboratory systems. Current versions operate in the fields of industrial robot control, the inspection of printed-circuit boards in electronics, etc. There are also several military applications.

A relatively recent development is the use of expert systems in education and industrial training. A system at the Stanford Research Institute International trains operators in the assembly of an air compressor. A spoken dialogue between the system and the trainee would proceed as follows:

System:	'Try to assemble the air compressor.'
Trainee:	'How?'
System:	'Install pump, install pump brace, install pulley, install belt housing cover. Ready for questions.'
Trainee:	'None.'
System:	'Install pump.'
Trainee:	'How?'
System:	'Get four $\frac{1}{4}$ inch long $\frac{5}{16}$ inch hexagonal bolts, and four $\frac{9}{16}$ inch flat washers, and four $\frac{5}{16}$ inch hexagonal nuts.'
Trainee:	'OK.'

etc.

The system can start at any point in a logical sequence of assembly steps and take the trainee to the desired objective—a fully assembled compressor.

Superficially, and in limited areas of application, some expert systems may appear to be highly intelligent. Indeed, there is good reason for this since their knowledge base is derived from recognized human experts. Some chess programs play a much higher level of game than novice players, and are 'caught out' only when encountering master-level opposition. Yet, they are slow, and make some surprisingly elementary mistakes. At the deeper level, the reasons for these shortcomings are clear: they are the three problems listed earlier. Expert systems are essentially computer models of human thought and they are only as good at *being original* as the psychological models employed by their programmers.

Further reading Michie, D. (ed.) (1979). *Expert Systems in the Microelectronic Age,* Edinburgh University Press.

11 Microforms

Introduction

Microforms offer a method of storage, retrieval and display of images recorded on microfilm. Other names used for this method include micro-image, optical storage and computer-fiche. The images to which the method is particularly well suited include documents and pictures, originally on paper, and computer-generated text and graphics, originally on a video screen. Microforms complement other computer storage media, computer display methods, and video recording and display techniques (video discs and cassettes) in administrative, financial, bibliographic and other applications.

Recording the images

The medium used for microforms is photographic film, usually 16, 35 or 105 mm wide. The first two are often in roll-film format, loaded into plastic cartridges or cassettes. The 105 mm film is usually cut into 148 mm lengths to produce flat microform or *micro-fiche*. A fiche contains an array of images, all of them much reduced versions of the original image. The reduction ratios in current use can vary between 18 and 48. Depending on this, the number of images on a fiche will be between 60 and 200. The now defunct *ultra-fiche* could carry up to 3000 images on the same area of film, at the reduction ratio of 150.

Images can be recorded either by conventional photographic methods, using flat-bed or rotary cameras, or directly from computer data in *computer-output microform* (com) devices. The essential features of a flat-bed camera are shown in Fig. 11.1. The reduction ratio can be

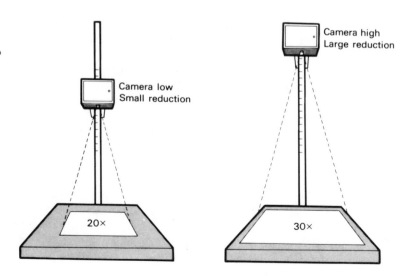

Fig. 11.1 Flat-bed microfilm camera. The reduction ratio is related to the distance between the bed and the film in the camera

Camera low
Small reduction

Camera high
Large reduction

20×

30×

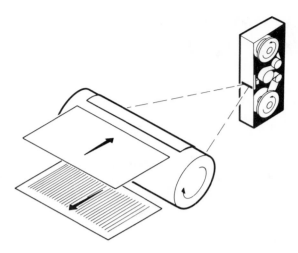

Fig. 11.2 Rotary
microfilmer

increased by raising the height of the camera over the bed which holds
the document to be photographed. A rotary microfilmer, as shown in
Fig. 11.2, is used for large production volumes. Both the original and the
film are moving when the exposure is being made, but the image is sharp
as the two movements are synchronized. The reduction ratio is varied, if
necessary, by changing the lens on the camera. In com equipment, the
image is produced by an electron-beam or laser controlled with great
precision by the computer. The equipment is effectively a microfilm
camera mounted in front of a video display screen. In newer models, the
film processing stage (dry processing) is also part of the equipment.

**Storage and
retrieval**

Microforms have gained acceptance both as a self-contained medium and
as part of computer-based information systems. In both cases, however,
the computer can be usefully employed to generate an index of the images
in terms of their content, and relate the indexing features of each image to
its roll or fiche number position. In some systems, the computer is also
used to mechanize the selection of a particular roll or fiche and its
presentation to the user.

In such computer-based storage and retrieval systems, the
microfilming of source images can be done in random order since the
computer takes care of the location of images on the basis of an 'address'.
Figure 11.3 shows the components and the inter-relationships of such
systems. The index to the information stored may be itself on microfilm
or it may be held within the computer and consulted by means of a video
display device.

In many systems, the retrieved images are viewed by means of a
specialized optical microfilm reader, which may also have an attached
(photographic) printer. It can take up to about 30 s to locate and display a
selected image in a computer-based microform 'library' (see Fig. 11.4).
More recently, however, the trend has been towards eliminating the
separate film reader–printer device and using the already present video
display unit for both computer and microform output. The principles
behind one such system are shown in Fig. 11.5. The images in this system
are held as a set of fiches in a carousel or as 105 mm roll film in

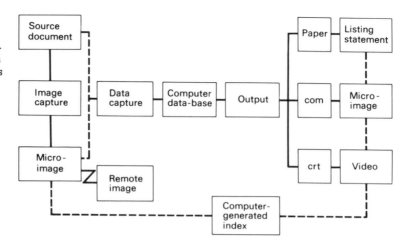

Fig. 11.3 Preparation of microforms and indices from a computer data-base. Computer-output microfilm (com) equipment generates the microforms; the cathode-ray tube (crt) screen is used to compose the index reference

Fig. 11.4 A commercial computerized microform retrieval system. The device on the left is the microfilm reader–printer, with computer below. On the right is the vdu. The system is suited to users with a need to process from 500 to 3000 documents per day. (3M United Kingdom Ltd)

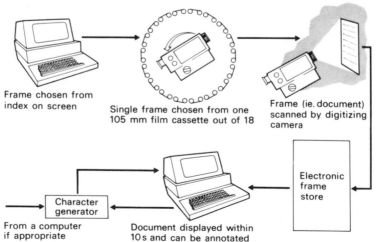

Fig. 11.5 A computerized system for video display of microforms. (After *Financial Times* 14 October 1980)

rapid-access cassettes. The image identified by a user from an index is converted to computer-coded data by a special camera. This camera scans the film to produce about 3.5 million picture points. The information on whether a point is black or white is placed in an electronic frame-store. From here, a digitized version of the image can be reconstructed on a video display, and the microfilm image released, possibly for another user. The process from identification to presentation is claimed to take about 10 s.

Since the image is now in digital form, it can be further processed. The system allows for annotating the image, say, bringing it up to date by means of a keyboard or a light pen, or by another computer. The image can also be transmitted as digital data to remote locations, perhaps by satellite. The updated image can be stored in microfilm form, after passing it through a com device. An interesting feature of this system is that the digitized image can be improved in quality to achieve a uniform, high technical level of presentation. Image-enhancement methods, first developed for the improvement of pictures from space flights, can be applied for this purpose. One version of this system is able to store 4 million frames, equivalent to 14 million million elementary items of data (black/white picture points).

Applications

Microfilm is said to have been invented during the Franco-Prussian War, to send reduced diagrams of troop positions by strapping these to the legs of carrier pigeons. Technical advances since that time have helped to reduce the size and the cost and to improve the quality of micro-images, but only the advent of digital technology has made it possible to transmit microfilmed information significantly faster than carrier pigeons had.

In between those two milestones in the history of microfilm, the 'bread-and-butter' application was in the financial world, more specifically in cheque transaction recording. Cheque processing machines store the complete images of cheques handled by a bank, and relate these to information stored as magnetic-ink characters on the cheque.

The main claims for microforms are based on two sets of advantages which they offer: saving in storage space and cost, and the ability to combine storage and display of data in one medium. Compared with paper, microforms indeed offer very considerable saving in space: the volume taken up by microfilmed versions of paper documents is estimated as less than 2 per cent of the volume of the documents themselves. As an example, the administration of the EEC currently involves the printing of 1.887 million sheets of paper a year, at a cost of £29m. About one-fifth of the publications is sent directly for storage. Change to microform would reduce both the cost and the volume of this stockpile—quite apart from giving an opportunity to re-assess its usefulness.

Microforms also provide access to source documents which would otherwise be not easily available; for example, historical documents, past copies of newspapers (*The Times* is now available on microfilm as far back as 1785), university theses, catalogues, etc. In this way, libraries and other documentation agencies can increase their holdings without the corresponding increase in shelf space and air-conditioning costs.

The second claim can be illustrated by an application of the computer-based system described earlier. In West Germany, police required a means of rapid identification of the location of car accidents. Detector devices mounted in cars would emit a radio signal when deceleration exceeds a certain limit. The signals are picked up by a network of receivers which help to fix the location of the accident. Associated computers turn this location into a map reference, and that in turn is used to retrieve and display a map section from a micro-fiche store. As the display is on a video screen, the map details can have superimposed on them the details (time, exact position, etc.) of the accident in the form of text.

The number and range of applications of microforms are influenced, apart from the usual factors of cost, reliability, etc., by their acceptability to users. Users of microforms do not handle the paper format of a document unless they obtain a print-out or copy of the micro-image. Normally, they would view the image projected onto a frosted-glass screen or displayed on a video screen. Reading text by these means, as opposed to reading the printed source documents, has been shown to lead to fatigue more rapidly (Spencer and Reynolds, *Factors Affecting the Acceptability of Microforms as a Reading Medium*, RCA, London, 1976). The same report also points to possible problems in the presentation of graphical material on microforms: the photographic or computer-image generation process can reduce the quality of halftone or colour pictures, and is currently best suited to the reproduction of line drawings.

Due to the difficulty of rapid 'flipping' from one frame to another, the presentation of material on the 'frames' becomes a crucial factor. The interrelation of text with tables, references, notes, etc., is a more important consideration when using a set of frames than in the layout of printed materials. The legibility of characters, the characteristics of the viewing screen, the annotation and indexing of the contents and the degree of user control over these all seem to affect the acceptability of microforms to a significant extent.

The next step in microfilm technology is likely to be the transmission of images stored on microfilm by facsimile. This will make it possible to extend electronic mail techniques to information systems and other large data bases in respect of graphical information.

Further reading

Ashby, P. and Campbell, R. (1979). *Microform Publishing*, Butterworths.
Kish, J. L. (1980). *Micrographics—A User's Manual*, Wiley.

12 Voice communication with computers

Introduction

Voice communication presupposes an ability to accept spoken information (*voice input*) and to produce comprehensible speech (*voice output*). A range of techniques is currently under development to enable people to use speech as direct input to computer-based systems, such as expert systems (see p. 91) or industrial automata. Computer-generated speech is already a feature of many commercially available information technology products. Eventually, both voice input and output are likely to be provided in information systems (see p. 121).

Voice input and output present a different set of problems to the information technologist. Therefore, we shall take them separately, looking at the less difficult task of voice output first.

Voice output

There are two main techniques of computer-controlled speech generation in current use: synthesis by *concatenation* and synthesis by *rule*.

Concatenation simply means the linking together and replay of previously recorded complete words and phrases. A well-known example is the speaking clock service offered on many large telephone systems: there the 'message' is made up of a limited number of stored phrases, put together automatically to form complete sentences. In more recent systems employing this technique, the stock of words and phrases enunciated by a human speaker is stored in digital form, rather than as direct-speech signals on tape. In other respects, however, the approach is the same: sentences are 'assembled', this time under computer control, from a limited set of pre-recorded elements.

The main problem with this technique is its unwieldiness for general applications where the number of words and sentences may approach the contents of a full-size dictionary. Also, since usually only one version of a word or phrase is stored, this precludes the variations of stress and intonation normally expected in natural speech.

Synthesis by rule overcomes these problems, but at the expense of complexity. Synthesis here refers to the assembly of words from their constituent elements, the *phonemes*. (There are about 45 of these in the English language, but other languages have a different number of different phonemes.) The computer stores a large number of empirical rules, to convert text to phonemes, phonemes to parameters of a model of the human vocal tract, and finally the parameters to voice. The parameters determine features like pitch and loudness of the elementary components of speech, and ensure the smooth transition from one to another.

Current systems employing concatenation employ a vocabulary of between 100 and 200 words. Those using synthesis by rule offer up to 64 phonemes on a single integrated circuit.

Voice input

The task here does not stop with the conversion of speech to computer-compatible form. This is a difficult enough problem because speech is represented by a complex, rapidly varying electronic signal, which gives rise to a vast amount of data to process. The challenging part comes in matching the spoken utterance to one of a wide range of possible, pre-stored words, phrases or sentences. This problem is made more difficult by the signals corresponding to a particular utterance being different from speaker to speaker, or even changing for the same speaker, when he or she is suffering from a cold, when in a highly emotional state, when very tired, etc. Moreover, an utterance does not necessarily correspond to one word or one sentence. Some people tend to run the words of a sentence together. So, the state-of-the-art in speech recognition requires the speaker to pronounce words with definite pauses between them, or else it starts with segmenting the speech on the basis of its acoustical features (see Fig. 12.1).

In the first case, words can be identified by the 'brute force' method of matching their complete acoustic signal against a stored set of these. The stored set, which can comprise tens of thousands of signal patterns, can be generalized for a wide range of speakers. Better performance, however, is obtained when the set is small and when it is 'tuned' to a particular speaker. This is achieved by the speaker recording all the possible words which the computer will later be called upon to recognize. Even so, voice input systems employing this technique are better at identifying a speaker, than the words pronounced by that speaker. This becomes a useful facility in applications such as the verification of bank account holders inquiring about the details of their account over the telephone. To set up the system, the account holder must first pronounce some words over the telephone, which are then stored and used later for identification on the basis of the voice pattern. This facility has been demonstrated by the Bell Laboratories in the United States.

Alternatively, acoustical features can be extracted from the voice signal and these matched, by the computer, against stored original templates. These features usually break speech down into shorter segments, equivalent to phonemes. The computer then combines the identified segments into words, the words into sentences, and so on. Linguistic information is also utilized as a means of verification of the syntactic and semantic validity of the computer's guess at what has been said.

Applications

There are several reasons why voice communication with computers is an eagerly awaited development in all areas of application of information technology. One is the expressed preference of users for this mode of interaction, as 'it makes the machine more human'. It has been shown by Chapanis and his co-workers at Johns Hopkins University that when two people cooperate on solving a problem they are about twice as efficient when they talk to each other as when they use other means of communication, such as handwriting, typing or visual signalling. It could relieve people from having to use a keyboard or concentrate on a visual display for long periods of time. It also frees an operator's hands (in, say,

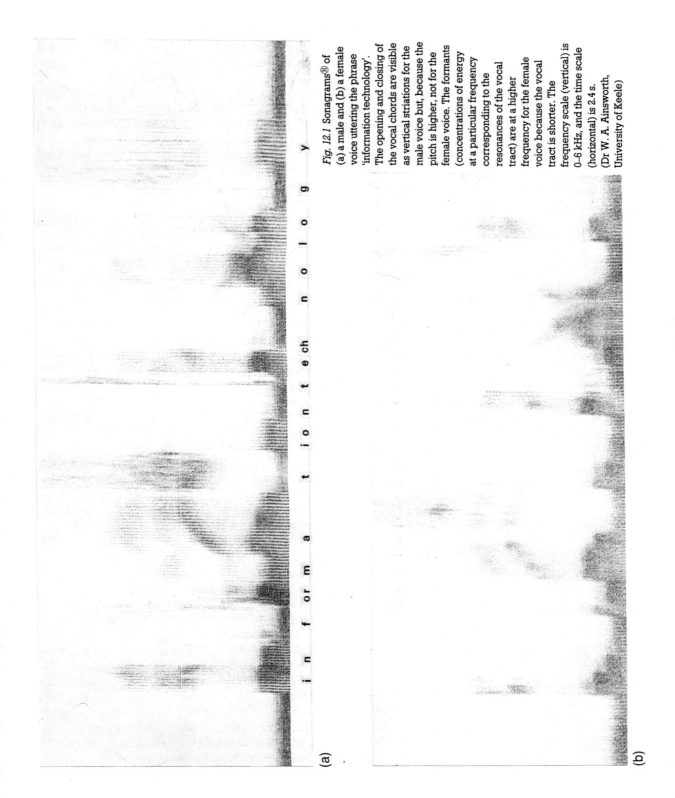

Fig. 12.1 Sonagrams® of (a) a male and (b) a female voice uttering the phrase 'information technology'. The opening and closing of the vocal chords are visible as vertical striations for the male voice but, because the pitch is higher, not for the female voice. The formants (concentrations of energy at a particular frequency corresponding to the resonances of the vocal tract) are at a higher frequency for the female voice because the vocal tract is shorter. The frequency scale (vertical) is 0–6 kHz, and the time scale (horizontal) is 2.4 s. (Dr W. A. Ainsworth, University of Keele)

sorting or inspection operations) from having to set switches, etc. Instead, he or she can issue spoken instructions to the machine.

For example, in mail sorting, the sorter simply tells the computer the destination of an item on a conveyor belt, and that item is automatically directed into the appropriate slot. In car assembly, the list of faults on a particular car can be produced by verbal identification as the inspector examines the car at the end of the production line. In some American cars, planned for 1983 production, it is intended to replace some warning lights with 'talking' equivalents (e.g. for low fuel level, or when the statutory speed limit is exceeded). Similar *hazard warning* functions are usefully performed by voice-output equipment in many different applications (e.g. on the shop floor or as part of a security system). Automatic *announcement* generation is also a current application. For example, pilots flying on international routes sometimes have problems in understanding weather reports spoken in English but with a heavy local accent. A voice-output device has been used to convert weather data into at least a consistent English accent.

In office, commercial and financial applications, voice communication can be a means of *data entry* to other, computerized equipment. In the longer term, the range of words or phrases handled by voice-input equipment can lead to the replacement of the keyboard in many applications. For the time being, however, the performance of speech-recognition equipment is too low for any but the most mundane operations. An important advantage of voice communication in this range of applications is its naturalness. That, in turn, reduces the time needed to learn to use any equipment which offers such a facility.

In communication, the *retrieval of information* from computerized data-bases over the telephone would be aided by voice-communication equipment. This would both accept spoken inquiries and answer in natural language. The voice-output aspect of this has already been put into practice. Voice output is also envisaged in the new generation of digital telephone exchanges, to inform users about the facilities available and to supplement existing information services.

In health care, voice output has an important role to play in reading devices for the blind, and as an aid for those with speech-production difficulties. Voice input and output would help blind people to interact with any computer-based equipment having these facilities.

In education, voice input and output can perform a useful role in language learning and translation. Devices are already available for checking spelling and for speaking a limited set of sentences in a variety of languages (intended primarily for people who travel to foreign countries). In domestic and consumer applications, there is already a range of electronic games, appliances and personal computer systems equipped with voice output. The applications, often not more than gimmicks, fulfil roles like announcements, operating instructions, audible warnings, etc. Voice input has also started to make an appearance in simple control operations for domestic electronic equipment. The mass market for such relatively trivial uses stimulates and supports work for other applications.

Further reading

Dixon, N. R. and Martin, T. B. (eds.) (1979). *Automatic Speech and Speaker Recognition*, Wiley.

Rabiner, L. R. and Schafer, R. W. (1978). *Digital Processing of Speech Signals*, Prentice-Hall.

13 Data networks

Introduction and fundamentals

The purpose of data networks is to interconnect computers and other devices which work with computer-coded data, so that data can be transferred from one location to another. As far as the user of information technology is concerned, data networks operate 'behind the scenes', but they exert a profound influence on the application of information technology. For example, access to remote information systems (see p. 121), the operation of electronic mail (see p. 117), and, increasingly, the world's telecommunication services (see p. 51) are all dependent on the transmission of digital data. The problems of setting up and operating data networks are essentially technical and economic ones, but the decisions being taken about these problems today are going to influence the progress of information technology for many years to come.

At first sight, there seems to be no good reason to distinguish between telecommunication networks and data networks. After all, they are both concerned with the transmission of signals representing information, and they both have the same origins: the public telephone and telex networks.

The signals which represent computer data are digital, or on-off pulses. The world's telecommunication network prior to the need for data transmission was built up to handle speech and telex signals, which reflect the information handling rates of people. As a result, a single-speech link is allocated a bandwidth (see panel on page 108) of about 3500 Hz on the public telephone network. The discontinuous variation of digital signals and the speed at which computers operate impose a completely different demand for bandwidth on the transmission channel. To illustrate this, consider the effect of sending data at two different rates on common computer operations, as shown in Table 13.1.

Table 13.1

Data to be transferred (using bit-by-bit, or serial, transfer)	Approximate number of bits	Transmission times	
		At 1.2 kbit/s	At 256 kbit/s
Video screen full of text	1–4×10^4	8–32 s	0.04–0.16 s
Floppy disc, 20 cm, double-density	5×10^6	65 min	20 s
Computer tape, 720 m reel	1×10^9	230 h	1 h
Facsimile page, black and white	2–6×10^5	2.5–8 min	0.8–2.4 s
Digitized speech, 1 s duration (pulse-code modulation)	6.4×10^4	1 min	0.25 s

The first transmission rate shown, 1.2 kbit/s, is what can be achieved, without resorting to complex and expensive techniques, on an ordinary public telephone line. Note, for example, that more than a few seconds' wait for a screenful of text is considered to be undesirable in most applications, while the 1 min transmission time of one second's worth of speech makes that transmission rate impracticable for speech. The second transmission rate of 256 kbit/s is what can be currently achieved on a local network designed specifically for data transmission. Satellite data-links are faster still, by a factor of about 100 if the complete channel is used for one message.

Apart from the different bandwidth requirements, the transmission of data on the conventional telephone network is inconvenient because it takes up the available channels for longer times than the average conversation (thus causing congestion), and because it is easily corrupted by line noise and other transmission problems. A considerable amount of technical ingenuity has gone into alleviating these problems, so that the highly expensive national and global speech telephone networks could be exploited for data transmission. Simultaneously, a start has been made by several countries on the creation of new networks for the transmission of data only, including digitized speech and tv signals.

Thus, at the present time, data networks may be based on the public telephone network, on private telephone lines leased from the national telecommunication network operators, or on a new generation of public and private transmission and switching networks established specifically for data communication. Eventually, we can expect data traffic to switch completely to the new facilities.

The simplest data network is one which interconnects a few pieces of computer equipment by lengths of wire or cable. This works quite well as long as:

(a) the distances involved are not large (a few hundred metres for a wire-pair, a few kilometres for a cable);
(b) the number of items of equipment is small (if each of them is to be able to communicate directly with all others);
(c) the transmission rates are relatively low (a few tens of kbit/s for wire, a few hundred kbit/s for cable);
(d) the items of equipment have all been produced by the same manufacturer (or are otherwise compatible).

This simple network is also constrained by the fact that, in many countries, legislation prevents the transmission of signals by other than the national telecommunication organization, beyond the user's premises.

When any one of these assumptions proves too constraining, it becomes necessary to examine commercial alternatives. Depending on how they cope with these problems, commercial data networks can be categorized as shown in Table 13.2.

Table 13.2

Distance	Long-distance and local networks
Interlinking	Circuit-switched, message-switched and packet-switched networks
Data rates	Narrow-band and wide-band networks
Compatibility	Standardized and non-standard networks
Ownership	Public, private and value-added networks

Long-distance networks

Long-distance networks are operated in most countries by state-owned telecommunication authorities (an outstanding exception to this is the United States). To overcome the problem of signal deterioration with distance, national and international data networks include signal regeneration equipment (repeaters) in their long-distance segment (trunk network), but the link to this segment from/to subscribers' premises is often just a wire-pair. The installation and usage costs of long-distance links are quite high, so a great deal of effort goes into ways of transmitting the maximum amount of data through the smallest number of long-distance links.

One approach is to share a data link (line) among several different pieces of equipment. A commonly used, efficient technique for this is *multiplexing* (see also p. 56). If the bandwidth (data rate) of the link is higher than the requirements of the individual senders and receivers of data, the successive characters of messages can be interleaved at the sender's end of the line and unscrambled at the receiver's end, as shown in Fig. 13.1. Thus, multiplexing aims to ensure that the capacity of the link is fully utilized. The interleaving and disentangling of the data elements is performed automatically by multiplexers placed at each end

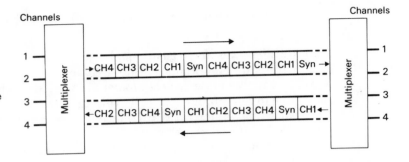

Fig. 13.1 A time-division multiplexer interleaves parts of messages from several channels for transmission along a bi-directional link. Synchronizing pulses at the end of each block of data ensure that the two multiplexers keep in step

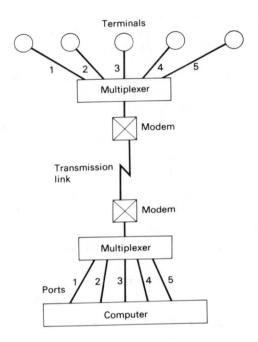

Fig. 13.2 In data transmission between a computer and distant terminals, the multiplexers ensure that the same link can be exploited by a cluster of terminals. Modems (modulator–demodulators) match the data signals to the link

of the line (Fig. 13.2). The current stage of development of such *time-division* techniques can ensure, for example, that a link operating at 9.6 kbit/s can be shared by over 100 pieces of equipment operating at 110 bit/s, or alternatively by a mixture of equipment using different data rates, and even a variety of computer codes.

A new generation of multiplexers has been recently introduced under the names of *data concentrators*, *network processors*, and *statistical multiplexers*. They include a mini- or microcomputer to improve the utilization of a line even further. The computer in this type of multiplexer detects when a sender or receiver which could be using the line is in fact not active, and allows either additional or faster-operating equipment to be connected to the line. The computer is also useful in detecting and correcting transmission errors and, in some cases, allowing data and non-digitized speech to be multiplexed on a line designed to transmit speech only. The cost of such equipment, however, has to be balanced against the costs of operating without it.

Local networks

Local-area data networks aim at interconnecting large numbers of different types of data equipment on a single site, for example, in a factory, office or university. An example of such a network is shown in Fig. 13.3. These networks are more recent in conception and execution

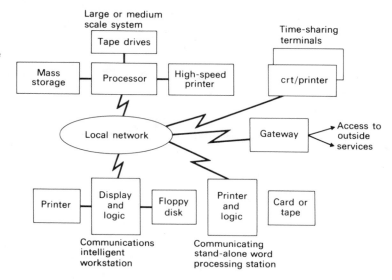

Fig. 13.3 A local network can interlink various items of computing and office equipment and can provide access to other public and private networks and computing and communication services

than the speech-oriented telephone network. They have been developed to deal specifically with data, and are faster, cheaper and less prone to error than the long-distance telephone network.

Local networks can be constructed along the same principles as long-distance ones, but on a smaller scale, and under the complete control of the user organization. Alternatively, they can be structured in the form of a *ring* or of a *broadcast network*. A ring layout is shown in Fig. 13.4. An example of a local ring-network is one developed at Cambridge University and known as the 'Cambridge ring'. It uses a twin wire-pair for transferring data at 10 Mbit/s (1 Mbit (megabit) = 1 million bits). The ring has been applied to produce an experimental office-automation

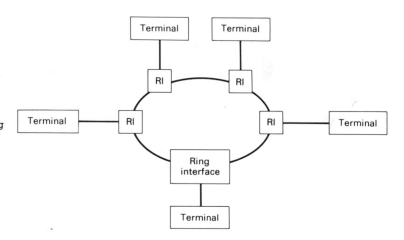

Fig. 13.4 In a ring-type local network, interface equipment is used to launch messages on the ring from terminals, to 'pick off' messages addressed to particular terminals, and to boost signals travelling in the ring

system, interlinking text processors and data-storage equipment. New equipment can be easily attached to the ring, up to a practical limit. At intervals, the ring needs to include signal repeaters to reshape the digital signals. This contributes to the virtually error-free performance of ring networks, but also to their cost.

The main strength of a ring network is its low error rate: less than one wrong received digit in 10 billion is claimed for the Cambridge ring. Its weakness is that it needs a repeater, or signal booster, at each point of attachment.

An example of the broadcast configuration is shown in Fig. 13.5. It has

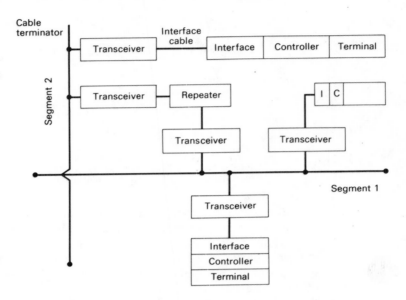

Fig. 13.5 In a broadcast-type local network, separate transmitter–receivers with repeaters are used to boost the signals

been developed by the Xerox Corporation in the USA, under the name Ethernet. The transmission medium is coaxial cable operating at the data rate of 1–3 Mbit/s. The network is extendable as it employs repeaters to regenerate the signals. Items of equipment (at the present time only of Xerox's own design) link to the cable through a transmitter–receiver unit, an interface and controller. These serve to select from the data travelling along the network only that portion which has been addressed to them. They also launch into the network data destined to other specific pieces of equipment.

A disadvantage of broadcast-type networks is that, because they are open-ended rather than formed into a closed loop, there is no confirmation that a message has been received, and there is no easy way of correcting transmission errors. By contrast, in a ring network, a message is 'read' by the addressee and is returned in its received form to the sender. If the sender is satisfied with this acknowledgement, it removes the message from the ring, otherwise it repeats the message.

In addition to these two types of local network, operating at data rates of up to 10 Mbit/s, and aimed at interlinking terminals and computers, wider-band local networks are also being introduced. One such network has a 350 MHz bandwidth, split into three segments: one handles 32 channels at 9.6 kbit/s and 16 channels at 64 kbit/s; the next one can take up to seven television channels; the third is a single channel of 12 Mbit/s data rate. This allows simultaneous digital speech, terminal-to-computer, computer-to-computer and television communication on a single coaxial cable.

At the time of writing, none of these types of local data network has been fully developed, and even less standardized or widely accepted. However, in the light of the importance of the office market, and the need to interconnect a wide variety of currently incompatible equipment, the technology and applications of local data networks are likely to grow rapidly.

Circuit-switched networks

When a large number of items of equipment is to be able to send and receive data, it becomes first uneconomical and then physically impracticable to provide a permanent direct connection from each piece of equipment to all others. This problem, of course, is not unique in data networks but arises in all telecommunication networks employing wires or cables. The traditional approach, in telephone and telex networks, is to link a limited number of items of equipment not to each other, but to a switching centre (exchange). There is only one connection from each item of equipment to the switching centre, resulting in a star-shaped network, called a *star-network*. The job of the switching centre is to establish a short-term link between any two lines connected to it. The existence of a temporary link between two (or more) parties is referred to as a *call*, while the path between the calling and called parties is known as the *circuit*.

In long-distance networks, switching centres themselves are interconnected, forming a *mesh-network*. In this way, a circuit can be established, on a temporary basis, between an increasing number of items of equipment around the world. While the call lasts, in circuit-switched networks, the circuit and some part of the switching equipment are completely dedicated to that call, i.e. they are unavailable for other calls, even though at some point in time there may not be any signals passing along the circuit. Circuit-switched networks are currently by far the most widely used means of data transmission.

Message-switched networks

Message switching aims to overcome the problem of engaged lines (or expensive peak-rate call charges), by allowing messages to be sent to and stored temporarily at the switching centre. The messages are then 'delivered' automatically by a call from the switching centre to the called party. For these reasons, message switching is often referred to as *store-and-forward*.

Message switching is usually employed in star and mesh-networks when some time delay between the origination and reception of a transmission can be tolerated. The switching centres in store-and-forward data networks are, in many cases, computers which can conveniently store digital data, monitor the availability of lines, and initiate transmission according to pre-programmed rules, and so allow a better utilization of network resources.

| **Packet-switched networks** | Packet switching is a relatively new technique in data networks, first proposed in 1964 in the USA, and now being introduced world-wide. It is close to message switching in principle as it employs computers to control the flow of data and does not provide a dedicated physical path between the sender and recipient. The technique, however, does not operate with complete messages, but rather with segments of them, broken up into blocks with a given maximum size, called data *packets*, or data *segments*, up to 512 bits long. Each packet carries the identification of the intended recipient and also data about the position of the packet in the sequence which makes up the complete message, as well as data which aid in the detection of transmission errors. A packet of data, together with such auxiliary control data is called a *datagram*. The datagrams are formed and 'unpacked' by computers which are local to the sender and receiver. In the network, switching computers examine the addressing instructions of each packet and determine the appropriate route for it. If necessary, because of congestion, packets can be stored at such switching *nodes*. As a result, there may be some delay in transmission, just as in a message-switched network, but usually not more than a fraction of a second. |

An important advantage of packet switching is that the rate at which data are sent by a piece of equipment need not be fixed. In other words, a sender can generate packets of data at a rate appropriate to its purposes. In this way, the available bandwidth of the transmission channel is continually re-allocated between users, to make most of an expensive investment. This is in complete contrast to circuit switching, where a circuit with a fixed bandwidth is allocated to a call, whether it is carrying data or not. (Keyboard terminals are estimated to be active for only one-eighth of the time of a call.) But this is not all: the technique allows for the recipient accepting data at a rate which suits it, so that devices with very different data rates can communicate with one another. This is something that is not possible in circuit-switched networks unless the devices themselves contain adequate 'buffer' storage. Examples of packet-switched networks are the international services such as the ARPA network, the Canadian Teleglobe, the British IPSS (International Packet Switching Service), the European Euronet and EIN (European Information Network), and national services like the American Tymnet and Telenet, the French Transpac, the British PSS, and the Canadian Datapac networks.

| **Narrow-band and wide-band networks** | The terms 'narrow-band' and 'wide-band' are ill-defined but they are usually taken to describe bandwidths below and above the telephone circuit bandwidth of 3500 Hz. |

For transmission by the telephone network, data must be converted into signals in this band of frequencies, by means of *modems* (*mo*dulator–*dem*odulators). Practical considerations constrain the data rates on the existing public circuit-switched telephone network to 1.2 kbit/s. The use of specialized data-encoding techniques and of non-switched telephone lines allows this limit to be raised to 48 kbit/s, but at considerable extra cost.

Higher data rates can be achieved over short distances in the local networks described earlier (up to 10 Mbit/s are currently in use). Long-distance high-rate data transmission is possible at the present time by combining a number of narrow-band channels, but the longer-term solution is the installation of a new wide-band network. This can carry not only computer data, but any other signals in computer-coded form, including digitized speech at the data rate of 64 kbit/s. Such developments are in hand in several countries, although the cost of replacing the existing telephone network is quite considerable, and can take several decades to accomplish.

A further possibility is the direct transmission of data at high rates via a satellite link. The current series of Intelsat 5 communication satellites has a usable bandwidth of 2300 MHz, but a ten-fold increase even on this figure is being contemplated over the next 15 to 20 years.

Announcements by various potential operators indicate that 47 different satellite networks based on 83 satellite services are planned to become operational during the 1980s. The first of these, Satellite Business Systems (SBS), went into service in 1981.

Standardization

Data networks can be set up by any user or commercial organization, either by direct interconnection of equipment or via long-distance links leased from telecommunication network operators. The flow of data in any network needs to be controlled to ensure that data are not lost in the network (e.g., because the receiving equipment is not ready to accept it) and that it is not corrupted during transmission. Unfortunately, different computer equipment manufacturers use different methods to control data flow across the interface between two items of equipment. The rules governing the initiation and maintenance of the flow of data do at least have a common name—they are called *protocols*. But that is where agreement ends among the various manufacturers.

Due to this diversity, it would seem to be an impossible task to transmit data between items of equipment not made by the same manufacturer. What saves the day is a generally accepted *recommendation*, called V24, for connecting modems to the public telephone network. (The United States' version is known as specification RS232.) These recommendations define a set of control circuits and the layout of standardized connectors, but only for modems up to 9.6 kbit/s data rates. A new set of recommendations has been recently put forward for data-flow control along public data networks. One of these, X25, plays the same role as V24, but in this case for packet-switched data networks.

The effect of these recommendations is to assure those who accept it that at least their items of equipment will be able to communicate at the *lowest hardware level*. However, even this does not guarantee that any item of computing equipment can communicate with any other via a data network. Different computer manufacturers use different codes, procedures, etc., for utilizing the data which arrive along the network. So, in the remote control of software tasks, e.g. the control of program execution or file transfers, the manufacturers of computing equipment still set their own individual protocols. What is required by users is a general-purpose network standard which allows the connection of any data device to the network and which controls the flow of data in the network. Unfortunately, a number of different organizations are trying to define such standards, and there is no agreement in sight, at the time of this writing.

Ownership of data networks

The lack of widely accepted standards is one of the main reasons for the proliferation of *private data networks*. The access to a private network is limited, and as a result a greater security of data is possible than on a public network. However, private networks are expensive to set up and operate. The ownership of long-distance networks is, therefore, in the hands of national governments or large corporations. They then either market the transmission facilities of the network to the general public or lease some part of the network to those wishing to set up a private network. An interesting development is the interlinking of local private networks with long-distance public networks and through them, possibly, with other local networks.

Recently, a third type of network has been started up in the United States, the *value-added network*. This is based on transmission facilities leased from public network operators but uses privately-owned switching computers. This enables the operators of networks like Tymnet and Telenet to provide facilities not normally available on public data networks, such as an electronic mail service. Whether such value-added networks continue in the longer term depends on the willingness of the owners and operators of public networks to add the extra facilities to their own service.

Applications

The annual growth rate of the volume of data transmitted along networks in Europe is currently estimated at around 20 per cent. Most of this growth is attributed to the use of computer-based information systems via the public networks. In the United States, and elsewhere, there is also increasing use of data networks by organizations which are themselves geographically distributed, for example, banks, large manufacturing, retail and administrative organizations, e.g. for bulk-data transfers. In the longer term, we can expect the full range of current telecommunication applications to be taken over by data networks, including voice communication, teleconferencing, electronic mail, electronic funds transfer and videotex.

Further reading

Davies, D. et al. (1979). *Computer Networks and Their Protocols*, Wiley-Interscience.
Martin, J. (1976). *Telecommunications and the Computer*, 2nd edn., Prentice-Hall.

14 Electronic mail

Introduction

Electronic mail is primarily an alternative to the conventional postal mail service. Additionally, it offers a range of new features based on the storing and processing abilities of computers (see p. 77).

The concept of electronic mail covers a broad spectrum of systems and services whose main common feature is that the messages are converted to electronic signals for the purposes of transmission. Thus the notion of paper as the medium of the message is discarded, and paper is not even considered to be necessary, in some systems, as the starting and final forms.

Input to, and output from, an electronic mail system can be via a video terminal, or word processor, with printer, a facsimile machine, or indeed any data terminal, including computer vision (see p. 83) and voice communication systems (see p. 101). Transmission of electronic mail requires a telecommunication network. The vast majority of electronic mail is transmitted as computer-compatible data, and travels along data networks. Computerized switching systems may offer electronic mail as one of a range of services.

Electronic mail systems to be considered here include telex, facsimile, communicating text processors, message-switched networks and computer-based message systems.

Telex-based services

Telex (short for *tel*eprinter *ex*change) is a service similar to the public telephone service, except that it carries teleprinter signals instead of speech signals. The signalling rate is 50 bit/s or 6.6 characters/s. Teleprinters, which are a combination of a keyboard and a printer, generate a paper record of both received and sent messages.

The telex network is well-established with over 1 million subscribers. It is also highly automated, and is under continuous development. Plans have been announced for a 'super telex' service under the name teletex (not to be confused with teletext, which is a British system for displaying broadcast text on modified television receivers—see p. 125). *Teletex* will be faster (probably working at 2400 bit/s) and have a larger set of possible characters than telex. It effectively amounts to a network of communicating text processors. The first such service is expected to start in West Germany and Sweden in 1981, and expanded later to other western industrialized countries. Telex is also being linked to computer systems to provide an augmented range of facilities. The Mailgram service in the United States, for example, can accept messages originated by teleprinters, computers or voice, for transmission along the Western Union telex network. The interfacing is handled by a computer, but the messages are delivered by hand from local offices of Western Union.

Facsimile services

Public telegraph offices are also being used in some countries, e.g. Britain, France, Japan, to send document facsimiles to private 'telefax' receivers. Facsimile services can utilize either the telephone or the telex network for transmission of a faithful copy of an original document. The signal for transmission is generated by automatically scanning the page to be sent. Present standards provide for 3.85 scan lines/mm. An A4 page under these (Group 2) standards takes 3 min to transmit. Alternative standards, offering higher resolution and much reduced transmission times, have been proposed, with recent systems taking less than 1 min to transmit an A4 page.

An example of a public facsimile system is the British Post Office's Intelpost service inaugurated between London and Toronto, Canada, in June 1980, and between 18 British cities in February 1981. A page of text or drawing is converted into a digital signal by a facsimile machine located in the post office at the London Stock Exchange. The signals are then transmitted first to a computer capable of storing up to 1000 pages, and from there, via a telecommunication link, to another computer located at the destination. In the case of Toronto, the link is made through a satellite. At the present time, the pages still have to be delivered to and collected from the two ends of the link, but even so it takes, on average, a few hours to get a page from sender to recipient, instead of a few days by conventional mail. British Telecom announced in 1981 a competing facsimile service called Bureaufax, with links to up to 15 countries.

An interesting point is the need for the storage computer in the transmission chain. Without the data store, there is a serious limitation to facsimile systems: the sender and receiver terminals are expected to operate simultaneously, one scanning, the other printing the page. But if the receiving terminal is busy or faulty the service comes to a halt. With the computer, the time-consuming process of converting the page to data signals can proceed continuously, and the messages batched for automatic transmission at the appropriate time.

Computer-based services

The common feature of telex and facsimile is the need for paper as the input and output media. Paper-less electronic mail is usually associated with computer-based electronic mail systems. *Communicating text processors* are an example of these. Text processors are essentially computers, and so offer not only facilities of keyed input and printed output (as in telex), but also aids to editing messages prior to dispatch, and the accumulation of received messages. Some manufacturers provide for the linking of their text processors to a local computer network, or to the public telex network, as well as directly to other text processors. In such installations, a one-page letter can be transmitted from one text processor to another in a matter of seconds, depending on the transmission medium used, and also on whether the receiving terminal is ready to deal with the message.

However, when text processors are required to communicate with non-compatible computers or with ordinary computer terminals, a *message-switching*, or *store-and-forward* system can be used (see also p. 113). The message switch is an 'interface' computer, which accepts messages directed at some other terminal or computer, and performs any necessary conversions on data to compensate for speed or code incompatibilities between the sending and receiving equipment. It also stores any messages which it cannot forward because the receiving terminal is busy or which can be sent at off-peak times. A recent development by IBM allows the message to be spoken rather than keyed. The voice input is converted into computer-compatible form, and is forwarded, or stored by the message switch, as necessary. As a rule, a message-switching computer is not used to provide general computational or text processing facilities, it is more like a policeman directing traffic at a busy intersection of 'data highways'.

There is, however, but a short step from text processors, communicating via a message switch, to a *computer-based message system* (cbms). The computer, or network of computers at the centre of a cbms, is now equipped to file and retrieve messages and offer text processing facilities. Therefore, it centralizes many of the text processing functions, allowing less sophisticated terminals access to electronic mail services. Computer-based message services can be offered on an in-house network, or they can be rented from a public-access network. *Videotex networks*, with message facilities, are an example of this type of system (see p. 125). An important advantage of a cbms is that it allows person-to-person, rather than terminal-to-terminal communication. This is achieved by means of identity codes which a person must use to retrieve mail from the system. The code may be entered from any terminal connected to the network, so a person is not constrained either by location or time from sending or receiving mail. Indeed, portable terminals connected through the public telecommunication network to a cbms offer the same freedom as a radio-telephone but with the added convenience of storing a message if the recipient is not available at the time of the call. Using the same analogy, messages can also be 'broadcast' on a cbms to all other users, or to a defined group, by providing the computer with a single 'copy' of the message and a list of addressees. A 'registered mail' facility notifies the sender when his message has been received. Some cbms, currently at the research stage, also allow the computer to generate messages (announcements, reminders, etc.) to be read by people or by autonomous programs.

Applications

The complete range of electronic mail is applicable to the office and business environments. Conversely, office and business applications currently represent the main thrust of marketing activities of the providers of electronic mail systems. Beyond that, and in the more distant future, the home user is likely to be the target of new electronic mail systems. In all these areas, there are three main applications where the initial impact of electronic mail is likely to be felt:

(a) an alternative mail service;
(b) a complement to the telephone service;
(c) an optional medium for holding meetings and conferences.

Electronic mail can already claim advantages in speed, reliability and convenience over conventional postal services. It is, however, a long way behind them in cost, general availability and psychological acceptance, in particular as far as the data protection aspect of the messages is concerned (see p. 86). But electronic mail has one overwhelming advantage over paper-based mail which is likely to affect the balance in its favour over the next few decades: information is essentially a weightless, media-independent commodity. To transfer conventional mail, it is necessary to produce and move vast quantities of paper. To transfer the equivalent amount of information by electronic mail, no physical material needs to be moved from one place to another, and the energy requirements are vastly smaller.

In relation to the telephone service, electronic mail does not depend on the simultaneous availability of both parties. Messages can be stored and then forwarded to the recipients, or retrieved by them, from any location, as long as they have access to the network. In some cases, there is also an advantage in there being a written record or follow-up to otherwise ephemeral telephone conversations.

Lastly, electronic mail is being promoted, particularly in the United States, as an alternative to travel for certain types of face-to-face business meetings or small conferences. Provided that the participants already know each other, and also when it is difficult to find a mutually acceptable time or place for a meeting, it is possible for them to make written contributions via a computer-based message system. These contributions are then instantaneously available to the other participants. The 'conference', or collaborative project, may then go on over a period of time. People may address their remarks to all others or only to a selected group. This is indeed a new medium for group interaction and rapid dissemination and publication of ideas, with opportunities for immediate feedback.

Further reading   *Electronic Mail: User Alternatives in the 1980s*, Mackintosh Publications, 1979.

15 Information systems

Introduction

'Information systems' is a non-standard term covering computer-based services which provide information in response to specific requests from users. There are two types of input to such systems: the data which they store in anticipation of requests, and the requests themselves. The data may be stored as references to documents, microforms, or computer-coded text, graphics, etc. The service may be offered on a local basis or via a telecommunication network. Here, we are not concerned with the communication aspects; they are largely covered in the chapter on data networks, p. 106.

Information systems may be operated by organizations for their own benefit or offered to the public on a subscription basis. An example of the latter is videotex (see p. 125). The output from an information service is either a document, or computer data presented, say, on a video display or as voice output (see p. 101).

The main purpose of an information service is to satisfy users' information needs. The way in which these needs are expressed largely determines the principles of operation of a particular information system.

Document and data retrieval

Perhaps the most straightforward request for information is when the user supplies a complete reference for a document. The job of the service then is to locate a copy of the document and deliver it to the user. This is usually referred to as a *document retrieval* service. It may be aided by computers in compiling the index to the documents in store, and in physically locating a required document (as in a computerized warehouse). More often than not, however, information needs are expressed in terms of a request for data, such as, 'How many computers are installed currently world-wide?', or 'What books have been published about information technology?' To answer such questions, reference must be made to records stored either in printed form or as computer-coded data. The first of these is often referred to as *information retrieval*, the latter as *data-base search*. Information retrieval itself may be preceded by a data-base search, when the index to the printed records is computerized.

The distinction between document retrieval and information retrieval, then, is whether the object of the search is a completely specified document, or whether it is either part of the contents of a document (e.g. a telephone number retrieved from a directory) or one or more documents satisfying a content-related inquiry.

Differences in systems

Computer-based information systems differ from one another in a number of important respects:

(a) the range of subjects or documents covered;
(b) the assumptions made about the users of the service;
(c) the input–output interface;
(d) the equipment used to store the data;
(e) the programs which assist in the input, indexing, storage, identification and output of data.

Example: Euronet-Diane

Euronet is a data network which was inaugurated in 1979 by the telecommunication authorities of the member countries of the European Economic Community (see Fig. 15.1). It is used to provide users in those

Fig. 15.1 Euronet in 1980

countries with access to the information system Diane (Direct Information Access Network in Europe).

The information available through the network is aimed at researchers, engineers, scientists, managers, economists, the legal and medical professions. The subject coverage is correspondingly broad, embracing bibliographical data in these areas (publications, documents, etc.), reference and handbook material (catalogues, directories, statistics, case-law, etc.), patents, compilations, from lists of research projects in Britain to lists of national defaulters in Italy. The data are held on the computers of various participating organizations which originally compiled the data-banks for their own use, or as a free-standing service. The network essentially acts as a publishing medium for these organizations.

Euronet-Diane is initially a private network, that is, users need to subscribe to the service, and the number of users is strictly limited. Users are assumed by the system to be able to formulate and carry out their own searches, while on-line to one of the participating data-bases. (These users may be, of course, the people with information needs, or they may be intermediaries who are specially trained information workers.)

The hardware interface to the system is the computer terminal, operating at speeds from 110 to 9600 bit/s. To specify a request, a user must formulate it in a 'command language' (this may be proprietary for older established data-bases, or a standardized version for new ones). One of the commands causes a display on the terminal of the allowed search terms. These terms can be combined so as to narrow the field of search. The outcome of the search may be one or more titles or abstract of publications, or some factual information. The data which can be accessed through this service is stored in conventional computer data storage devices—magnetic disc units.

Type and range of inquiries

Although most information systems are effectively sophisticated filing systems, the use of computers contributes a range of features not normally found in manual filing systems. These features are based on the processing abilities of computers, which in this case are exploited alongside their capacity for data storage. Perhaps the most important of these features is the type and range of inquiries with which they are able to cope. This, in turn, is largely determined by the *search strategy* adopted in the system.

Some systems are specifically aimed at giving rapid response to anticipated types of inquiry. These include, for example, airline reservation systems, where inquiries may relate, say, to the availability of seats on specific flights. Current videotex systems, such as Prestel, are also of this type, although this may not be apparent at the first glance. For example, a user may wish to know about restaurants in a certain part of London. Information is organized in the data-base in the form of a search tree (see the section on videotex, p. 126 for more detail), and in making choices at various points (e.g. which part of London?) the *system* tells the *user* what questions it is able to answer. That is, the inquiry has been subtly transformed from the one which the user had in mind, to the one which the suppliers of information anticipated as being of general interest. By this 'sacrifice' such systems can give rapid service to a large number of inquirers.

At the other extreme, certain information systems allow for inquiries formulated in natural or slightly constrained language (the latter is usually referred to as a *query language*). The first task of the system is to convert the user's way of expressing an information need to one which the computer can handle. In some cases, this involves the language processing program asking questions of the user to remove ambiguities from the original formulation of the question. The program also warns the user if a particular question would require a lengthy search. The response is put together by the system after examining a very large number of stored records and extracting from them the relevant information—a time-consuming process for even well-structured storage systems. In most current systems of this type, the search is performed by a program, although ICL in Britain recently introduced the *content-addressable file store* (cafs) which searches by hardware, and therefore potentially more rapidly.

Programs are used also to assist with the original entry of data into the data-base—a vital process since it determines the ease with which the data can be later retrieved. Some of these programs automatically scan the text, looking for certain keywords and recording them, together with the context in which they occur; others automatically classify new data in terms of the keywords or other attributes. Yet others check the users' authority to make use of the system.

Although the general-purpose electronic digital computer is at the heart of the current generation of information systems, a considerable amount of research is going into new developments, such as the design of computer structures specially aimed at dealing with data structure and retrieval (data-base machines), and devices which are optical, rather than electronic methods for recording and searching for data (e.g. holographic stores and optical computers).

Applications

Information systems aimed at dealing with inquiries in anticipated form are employed in many operational situations. These include, for example, in communication, telephone directory inquiries; in finance and commerce, bank balance inquiry systems; in industry, production control and parts storage systems; in administration, police emergency systems. The common feature of these applications is the need for rapid response from the system. There is another set of applications, where the response time is measured not in seconds, but in minutes, and possibly in hours. These information systems aid in strategic decision-making, planning (e.g. management and government information systems), non-time-critical research and investigative work, statistical, archival and reference applications, where inquiries are random and unanticipated in form.

Further reading

Chorafas, D. N. (1980). *Data Communications for Distributed Information Systems*, Petrocelli Books.

Katzan, H. (1979). *Distributed Information Systems*, Petrocelli Books.

Lancaster, F. W. (1978). *Toward Paperless Information Systems*, Academic Press.

van Rijsbergen, C. J. (1979). *Information Retrieval*, 2nd edn., Butterworths.

16 Videotex and teletext

Introduction and fundamentals

Videotex or *viewdata*, as generic terms, apply to interactive (two-way) systems for transmitting text or graphics stored in computer data-bases, via the telephone network, for display on a television screen. This description, however, can equally well apply to the use of a time-sharing computer or of a specialist information system (see p. 121) via a data network, or indeed to some forms of electronic mail (see p. 118). What distinguishes videotex from these systems is that it is specially intended as a simple-to-use, low-cost information system, catering for large numbers of users.

Teletext is a non-interactive (one-way) form of videotex, that is, a method of transmitting text or graphics stored in a computer data-base, as part of broadcast transmissions, for display on a television screen. Again, it is intended for wide public use, carrying information of broad public interest.

Videotex and teletext systems have a similar structure, as indicated in Fig. 16.1. The hardware of each consists of a central data-base computer

Fig. 16.1 The main components of videotex and teletext. User terminals link to the data-base computers via the telephone network for videotex, and via broadcast channels for teletext. Only videotex has the reverse link allowing direct communication with the computer

(or several such computers), linked to a large number of television displays via a telecommunication network. The software for both includes a data-base storage and retrieval program operating on an organized set of textual and/or graphic data. The data are organized as 'frames', each containing a screenful of alphabetic, numeric and graphic symbols. The format of the frame, and the transmission codes for the characters are virtually the same for the two systems, at least for systems used in any one country.

The human element also tends to divide into the same groups for both systems: on the one hand, the users (the general public) and, on the other, the 'information providers' (organizations or individuals who supply the contents of the data-base). Other interested parties include the operators of the systems, and the suppliers of the various technical components.

Videotex and teletext differ, however, in the way they transmit the data and also in the way the user controls what data are to be displayed.

Videotex systems

Videotex systems assume that the user has a telephone, to which a tv monitor or television set can be connected, via an electronic interface internal or external to the set. The interface usually includes a control keyboard, a modem (for converting data signals to and from the form used for telephone transmission), an auto-dialler (for calling the data-base computer and identifying the calling terminal at the press of a button) and circuitry for generating the displayed picture from the received data. There may be also provision for connecting a printer and/or some recording device so that received frames may be stored by the user.

The user selects a frame to be displayed by pressing keys on the keyboard. Each frame is identified by a unique code and this can be keyed in directly, if the code is known to the user. Alternatively, a set of choices, in terms of subject break-down, lead the user to a particular information frame. Various indices, presented as frames in the system, also help in selecting an information frame. In some systems, the keyboard may be used to gain access to the data-base by typing in a keyword, to discover what data are being stored on a particular subject.

Teletext systems

Unlike videotex, teletext systems do not employ sound-coded signals travelling within the relatively narrow bandwidth of telephone circuits. Instead, the coded character signals are sent as part of television picture signals. On a 625-line tv system, the data transmission rate is just under 7 Mbit/s. However, this rate is not sustained: in most teletext systems, data transmission occurs only in bursts. The duration of the burst is some fraction of the time it takes to transmit one tv picture. For example, the Ceefax and Oracle teletext systems in use in Britain transmit data at this rate for about one ten-thousandth of a second, 50 times a second. The full data rate would be available only if no tv picture were transmitted simultaneously with the teletext transmission.

In the British teletext systems, different sets of frames are transmitted on a 'carousel' basis. This means that each complete set of frames, held in the data-base, is transmitted, one frame after another, in a continuous cycle, just as a carousel-type slide projector would show slides if placed under automatic control. Each set of frames in a 'carousel' is transmitted on a different broadcast channel.

The reason for this mode of operation is that a user cannot signal to the computer which frame he or she wants to view, since the broadcast channel is one-way—from the central transmitter to the receivers. As in videotex, each frame is identified by a code, and the user is supplied with an index which briefly describes the content of each frame. Combined television–teletext receivers offer the user a set of switches or keys which can be set to the code designating a particular frame. When that frame is transmitted in the sequence frames, electronic circuitry in the set identifies its code and stores the data which make up the frame. It also converts the data signals into a viewable picture which is retained on the screen until the computer changes the contents of that frame. In order to reduce the waiting time for a particular frame, the number of frames in the 'carousel' must be rather limited. For example, to keep the maximum waiting time to less than 30 s, the British teletext systems work with less than 200 frames.

Frame content

In both videotex and teletext systems, the content of any particular frame can be changed while the system is in operation. In videotex, a user will receive the contents as they exist at the instant when the user's selection is made. In teletext, a fixed selection setting will present the new contents of a selected frame when that frame next comes around in the 'carousel'. In this way, for example, news flashes and other 'instant' information can be received as it is keyed into the computer's data-base, or 'sub-titles' to a tv program can be produced, super-imposed on the tv picture.

Developments and compatibility

Videotex and teletext systems are under continuous development. Moreover, there are several different, technically incompatible systems being developed in different countries, with no clear standard emerging at the time of writing. The three main contenders are the European (Eurotel), Canadian (Telidon) and Japanese (Captain) standards. Proposals combining features of the European and Canadian systems have been put forward in the USA.

The Eurotel standard for videotex receivers was agreed in 1981, as a compromise between the initially somewhat different British, French and German systems.

Prestel (British videotex system)

Prestel, the world's first public videotex service, started its market trials in 1978. Public service began in 1979, followed in 1981 by an international service.

A Prestel frame is made up of 960 character positions in a 24 row, 40 column array. Each position may be filled by a text character or a graphic rectangle. The graphic rectangles in turn are broken down into 3 rows of 2 smaller squares, each of which may be either dark or coloured. Low-resolution graphics can be made up from combinations of such rectangles. For obvious reasons, this is referred to as a 'mosaic graphic' facility. A character or graphic rectangle may take any one of seven colours, with a different coloured background, if required. Characters may also be doubled in height and made to flash. The coded frames are held in magnetic-disc stores in a network of computers distributed around Britain. Data are transmitted from the computers to the users at 1200 bit/s, from the users to the computers at 75 bit/s.

At the time of writing, each of 180 000 frames is replicated at 18 computer centres. Plans include the storage of 200 000 most frequently used pages, of local and national relevance, at each centre. A central 'data warehouse' would store the less frequently requested frames. Another planned feature would allow a sub-area of each frame to be occupied by a higher-resolution graphic. A recently announced new facility will enable users of Prestel to gain access to a wide range of computer-held data-bases and information services via a 'gateway'—a standardized computer-communication link controlling the flow of data between the 'host' computers and the videotex network.

Antiope (French videotex and teletext standard)

Antiope* is a combined videotex and teletext standard. A videotex service based on it, called Teletel, came into operation in 1981. It is in many ways similar to Prestel, with the following main exceptions:

(a) a larger set of possible text and graphic character attributes is used (each character being defined by 16 bits rather than by 7 bits as in Prestel), in a 40-row 25-line mosaic;

(b) to compensate for the larger amount of data to be transmitted, the system was designed to send data at the higher rate of 2400 bit/s, instead of the 1200 bit/s of Prestel;

(c) plans include the use of packet-switched data transmission in the videotex mode, and the broadcast transmission of selected frames from a common data-base in teletext mode (the common data-base may include a range of public or private information systems).

Telidon (Canadian videotex and teletext standard)

Telidon was first demonstrated in 1978, and small-scale field trials started in 1980. Telidon is different from both Prestel and Antiope in the way graphic images are built up in a frame. Instead of a mosaic of small squares, pictures are composed of basic graphic elements—points, lines, arcs, polygons and rectangles. This 'alpha-geometric' method of frame coding is capable of providing more detail, but at the expense of greater complexity (and higher cost) in the circuitry of the television receiver than the 'alpha-mosaic' approach of the European systems. However, the Telidon standard permits a trade-off in the complexity of the receiver and the quality of the displayed picture. It also makes the design of the computer-end of the data-base independent of technological developments in receiver design.

An alternative, 'photographic' display mode is also available on Telidon, to cater for images which are not conveniently expressed in terms of geometric elements (e.g. the human face or signatures). This mode is rather like the mosaic method of the two previous systems, but with a higher resolution, and therefore requiring more data to be transmitted for each full picture. It is transmitted point-by-point, just like a facsimile picture.

Captain (Japanese videotex system)

Captain (Character and Pattern Telephone Access Information Network) is one of several experimental public information systems for Japan, and is being planned to go into service from 1983. Like the 'photographic' mode of Telidon, its pictures are made up of an array of dots (192 rows by 240 columns). This caters for the display in any one frame of up to 480 of the 3000–4000 possible Kanji, Hiragana and Katakana characters of

*Antiope stands for Acquisition Numerique et Televisualisation d'Images Organisées en Pages d'Ecriture (digital acquisition and tele-display of pictures organized as written pages)

written Japanese. The relatively high resolution picture requires an increased data rate compared with other systems—up to 4800 bit/s. Captain is intended for operation via the public telephone network.

Applications

Apart from their role as information services, teletext and videotex can be considered as potential distribution media for all kinds of digitally-coded data. One natural candidate for this type of application is *computer software* (see p. 78). Experiments have confirmed the possibility of receiving, from a central 'computer program repository', packaged programs via videotex or teletext, storing it in a user computer, and then making use of it in a self-contained mode. This application of the new media has been referred to as *telesoftware*. Other data so transmitted into people's homes could include electronic mail, electronically published newspapers, books, educational materials, etc.

Videotex, being a two-way medium, is particularly suited to electronic mail (message sending) applications. At the present stage of development of computer, telecommunication and data-network technology, however, a truly large-scale person-to-person electronic mail service involving millions of subscribers is not a realistic proposition.

On a smaller scale, though, within large organizations or on a limited subscription basis, an electronic mail–videotex network is quite feasible. Private videotex services have been built to demonstrate this feasibility and to explore the potential of this medium. The British Open University's Optel system is an example of such a network. A line of future development, linking the smaller networks via data 'gateways', offers an evolutionary way towards an international electronic mail and information system. In some countries, particularly in North America, a different line of development is possible. There, significant investment is being made into cable-tv, including two-way cable. This may provide an alternative data pathway to the traditional telephone network. Thus, a combination of teletext (rather than videotex) and cable-tv systems can lead to a competitive range of facilities for the users, including, for example, mail order or 'yellow pages' directory information.

In the final count, the method of delivery of the data (whether by telephone, broadcast, cable or satellite) is less important than the quality of information and the services which become available to very large numbers of people in a cost-effective way. As noted in earlier chapters, some possible services are already being explored on a smaller scale as 'add-on' options to the telephone service: electronic mail, banking, publishing, etc. As to the quality, range and cost of the information, these are likely to be the main determinants of the pace at which this new mass communication medium develops.

General reading on information technology

Advisory Council for Applied Research and Development (1980). *Information Technology*, HM Stationery Office.

Arden, B. W. (ed.) (1980). *What Can Be Automated?*, MIT Press.

Chartrand, R. L. and Morentz, J. W. (1979). *Information Technology Serving Society*, Pergamon.

Dertouzos, M. L. and Moses, J. (1979). *The Computer Age: A Twenty-Year View*, MIT Press.

Martin, J. (1978). *The Wired Society*, Prentice-Hall.

Westley, A. (ed.) (1979). *Convergence: Computers, Communication and Office Automation*, 2 vols, Infotech.

Whisler, T. L. (1970). *Information Technology and Organizational Change*, Wadsworth Publishing Co.

On the applications of information technology in the office

Cecil, P. B. (1980). *Word Processing in the Modern Office*, 2nd edn, Benjamin/Cumming Publishing Co.

Westley, A. (ed.) (1980). *Office Automation*, 2 vols, State-of-the-Art Report, Series 8, No. 3, Infotech.

Communication

Hills, P. (ed.) (1980). *The Future of the Printed Word*, Frances Pinter.

Health and education

Deland, E. C. (ed.) (1978). *Information Technology in Health Science Education*, Plenum.

Afterwords: the future of information technology

ELLEN A. LAZER
Senior Editor, Knowledge Industry Publications, Inc.

A revolution in communications began in the middle of the nineteenth century with the telegraph, joined in later decades by the telephone and radio and television broadcasting. By the middle of the twentieth century, computer intelligence had made possible the rapid, precise manipulation of messages tailored to many individuals. Now we are in the midst of dozens of fundamentally new information technologies, all based on computers, telecommunications and data networks: electronic mail, information systems, cable tv, video-tape and disc systems, videotex and teletext, and more.

Today a businessman can buy a communicating word processor for his department, commit his company's future to operating a database information service, obtain a language translater for himself and a teaching computer for his children. What does this all mean?

The preceding chapters of this book have introduced and to some extent defined the industry of electronic communications. They describe the current concepts, applications and tools of information technology, distinguishing between established applications and those still on the magnetic drawing board. The non-technical reader has in this book the opportunity truly to understand the nature of the new technologies that are affecting him—their purposes, systems and transmission media. He can understand, for example, how and why a switched network can make possible a mass videotex service.

Information concepts and technologies, and the inventions that they lead to, are changing rapidly and are affecting every business and occupation and many fields of study. These changes are transforming the internal workings of all manner of institutions, affecting their budgets and productivity measures, and not least the careers of those responsible for departments ranging from data processing to finance. These changes are challenging such giants as AT&T, IBM and Xerox; providing grist for the mill of new high technology ventures; and deeply concerning such established institutions as broadcasting, print publishing and libraries.

Information technology is occupying the legal, regulatory and political forces in every nation because of the questions it raises about the content of and access to information, privacy, security, use and possible abuse. These implications have to be considered every time a new invention hits the marketplace or is announced in the business pages or flashes across the video display terminals.

The effects of information technology

While noting that the information landscape will not remain for long quite as it is pictured in this book, let us highlight some general conclusions about information technology:

—Information technology is changing the way we communicate and reach decisions.

—Information technology is changing the way we perceive the world—on the one hand making it more accessible, on the other making it more complex.

—Central to information technology is the computer. Its ability to store and process vast amounts of data at high speed makes the computer a threat to centralized control. But this awesome ability is being coupled with microcomputers that are making this power more accessible to more people.

—A significant and probably irreversible migration to information-related jobs is happening in the workplace.

—Technology-driven products have to find uses and users; a key question is how can they best complement human information handling.

—The need to examine the cost and value of information is becoming more apparent. Possession of information is becoming a matter of personal and professional importance, and vast information resources are potentially available to individuals.

—It is not enough to understand the engineering of information transmission; one must ensure the quality of information. Information must be reliable, accurate, verifiable, up to date, complete, precise, intelligible and relevant.

—The value of information is not inherent or constant, but depends on the needs of the recipient and the use to which it is put.

—The cost of information consists of the intellectual labour needed to generate it, and the methods and materials needed to process, store and distribute it.

Some specific predictions

—Telecommunications will prosper, as a result of the greater use of digital wideband networks and computerized telephone exchanges.

—Voice input and output are likely to be provided in future information systems.

—Optical communication, one of the newest technologies, will be greatly used in data networks, picture telephone, videotex and advanced facsimile.

—Microforms will continue to be of great use in banking and for access to source documents.

—Electronic mail will have an immediate impact in business, and much later in the home.

Applications: how information technology is used

The range of activities in which information is used is so abundant that the range of applications of information technology must be so, too. Information technology tools represent alternatives to established media and facilities: electronic signals, rather than words on paper, are transmitted, filed, modified or displayed. Much debate centres around whether the alternative offered by information technology is a solution to recognized problems or an answer in search of questions.

It is perhaps easiest to understand the basic notions of information and data, and the particular systems described in this book, when they are put to some use. The preceding chapters delimit the main applications, and some of the techniques and systems, in such areas as the office, manufacturing, finance, communication services, health care, education and training, and the home. The author suggests that information technology has proven its need in banking, communications and the military, where the amount of information or the time available for its processing makes electronic manipulation necessary. It has yet, he feels, seriously to affect the home, medicine and education, while the technology is 'on trial' in the office, manufacturing industries and commerce.

Office of the future

It has been noted that there are 20 trillion pages of paper stores in US offices, and that this amount is growing rapidly. Thus information technology has affected the most jobs, generated the most capital investment and received the greatest amount of attention in the office. What the office of the future aims to do, in a nutshell, is to offer new electronic media to supplement or replace traditional media and related equipment, and to integrate some of the functions and automate some of the tasks.

Down the road, we may expect computer-readable handwritten text and conversion of spoken words into digitally represented text. Earlier on the scene will be faster, higher-resolution facsimile services. The ubiquitous telephone, however, is not soon to be replaced (though its network will be), because machines are far from accomplishing automatic speech recognition. And the highly advertised 'integrated' office will depend strongly on development of local office networks, because the current machines are neither standardized nor compatible.

Communication services

There will be a fundamental revolution in communication services by the end of the century. Computers are being introduced into telephone exchanges and even into telephones themselves. We are beginning to see such new facilities as abbreviated dialing, repeat last call and call waiting. Telephone conference is commonplace in large organizations. Programs are being relayed by satellite and cable, and computerized databases are making possible the concept of 'a universal storehouse of knowledge'.

The home

The role of information technology in the 'home of the future' is a big question mark. Most homes have telephones, more are being wired for cable every month, and anyone can buy a citizens band radio, video cassette recorder or personal computer. A consumer can use his telephone to access a database, and scores of experiments are looking at whether consumers want and will pay for teletext and videotex services. The home computer will link up with other computers, to perform such functions as text processing, electronic mail, electronic funds transfer, home security and electronic shopping, but the usefulness—and economic justification—of such interlinking of domestic appliances has yet to be proved, as this book cautions.

The future of computers and data networks

Present-day computers operate at speeds of up to 30 million instructions per second, and their power limits are being reduced through data networks. Practical restraints, such as cost, reliability and physical size, do remain, however.

The usefulness of computers in information technology is determined by the extent to which people find tools based on them to be helpful and accessible. Their future includes: the rise of low cost, high power micros; higher density storage media (for example, a credit-card-sized piece of plastic that can hold 40 million bits of data, or about the content of ten books); and new storage methods such as bubble devices and holograms. In the research and development stage are concepts like computer vision, being used for simple automation tasks, expert systems (computer programs that give advice) and artificial intelligence.

Questions about the extent of computer-driven communications change remain: will computers really be used as 'expert consultants' and teachers? Will they read to the blind and caption for the deaf? Will they provide our main source of news and entertainment? These activities are being performed today on a limited basis; much needs to be done before these applications become cost-effective.

Behind the scenes looms the vital data network, which connects computers to transfer data. Eventually, the author expects, we will switch from existing telephone lines to a completely new generation of networks established specifically for data communications. The rise of value-added networks such as Tymnet and Telenet should be watched with interest.

Conclusion

Most of the ideas in this book are in or will reach the marketplace in one form or another. Explosive change is occurring in information technology, and there will be spectacular business opportunities. The information age is being realized in large business offices, and in the next decade will invade even the smallest firms. Then will come the mass 'consumerization' of high technology information services the marketers are guessing about and clamouring for. Some of the questions to be investigated include:

—How rapid and extensive will implementation of these services be? Who will be the early buyers? Who will they communicate with before such services are widespread?

—How will people acquire the skills needed to operate computerized database services or videotex? How effective are self-teaching computer programs? What skills do people need now?

—How much value will consumers place on electronic information services? Which services do they want or need?

—Is open competition—or government support and regulation—the best way to move forward?

—Will governments electronically monitor individuals?

—Will consumers feel the effects of 'information overload'? How can we recognize it?

—How will old telecommunications equipment co-exist with new?

—Where will the large chunks of capital needed for new equipment come from, without guaranteed returns?

—In what ways will a computer-literate society be different from today's society?

—How is the author/editor's role in data preparation changing? How is the material being redesigned for videotex, and indexed for computer access?

—What are the advantages of a worldwide information exchange network?

—Is electronic information transfer restricting or facilitating the flow of information? What role will the printed word play in the year 2000?

We have come a long way from the telegraph and Babbage's Analytical Engine. Perhaps future generations will see our information tools as similarly crude, but no one can accuse today's scientists of standing still.

Index